BLOOMSBURY PUBLISHING
Bloomsbury Publishing Inc.
1359 Broadway, New York, NY 10018, USA
50 Bedford Square, London, WC1B 3DP, UK
Bloomsbury Publishing Ireland Limited,
29 Earlsfort Terrace, Dublin 2, D02 AY28, Ireland

First published in the United States 2025

ISBN: HB: 978-1-63973-391-0; EBOOK: 978-1-63973-392-7

RY OF CONGRESS CATALOGING-IN-PUBLICATION DATA IS AVAILABLE

2 4 6 8 10 9 7 5 3 1

Typeset by Westchester Publishing Services

Printed in the United States at Lakeside Book Company

ut more about our authors and books visit www.bloomsbury.com
and sign up for our newsletters.

ury books may be purchased for business or promotional use. For
tion on bulk purchases please contact Macmillan Corporate and
mium Sales Department at specialmarkets@macmillan.com.
t safety-related questions contact productsafety@bloomsbury.com.

Cry for
Argent

My Life as a Faile

Tamara

BLOC

All ri
transmit
recording
prior pe
any way
(AI) tec
expressly
per A

LIBR

To find

Blooms
inform
Pr
For produ

BLOOMSBURY

NEW YORK · LONDON · OXFOR

For Mom, Dad, and Natalia

CONTENTS

PART IV: . . . AND BACK TO THE UNITED STATES

AUTHOR'S NOTE

The names of all individuals mentioned in this book, except celebrities and other public figures, have been omitted or fictionalized. Any resemblance between a fictionalized name and a real person is coincidental.

An Introduction to This Book (and to My Therapist, Betty Bakalman)

A few months ago, as I was close to finishing this book, and even closer to turning forty, I stopped to seriously think about whether I wanted to have kids. Did I want to bring a baby into this grotesque, pungent world? Did I want to be responsible for a child's security and stability when I had only recently started to feel secure in my own skin? I quickly decided that I was about 95 percent sure I did *not* want kids. Fuck that. The decision had been made.

A few days later, however, the 5 percent of me that *did* want kids started to rear its Accutane baby, cone-like head. Suddenly, that 5 percent began weighing on me so heavily, it felt like I was lugging around a pair of truck nuts made of steel. So I decided to see a therapist who could help me sort out this predicament.

The psychologist I saw was recommended to me by my filthy rich, great-aunt Chichi, who smokes like a machine and suffers from borderline personality disorder (just like most of the women in my family, whom you'll become acquainted with throughout this book). The therapist's name was Betty Bakalman, and she lived in Buenos Aires, Argentina, the place where I was born. Zoom made it possible for me to get treated by someone in Argentina, and I was thrilled about the idea because it was a way to feel closer to my country of birth. A country I've been crying over since I was a little girl.

The first thing I noticed about my new therapist was that she was always sweating. She was in her mid-eighties and wore a thick pearl necklace around her crepe-skinned neck. She could never manage to get her entire face in the Zoom frame. One time, I had to ask her to pull her chair back because she was sitting so close to the camera, I found myself telling some of my deepest secrets to her nose. Secrets like the fact that, as a young adult, I was so depressed from working as a Spanish interpreter at a hospital, where all I did was repeat what other people said all day, that I became addicted to painkillers. Imagine what it felt like to tell a giant nose on my screen that I was so out of it from the pills that, on one occasion, I mistakenly filled my car's gas tank with motor oil.

I know I'm not selling any of you on taking on Betty as a therapist, but I have to say that she really *did* help me. Maybe it was because she was hard of hearing, which required that I basically yell out my fears about motherhood. "I think I'm scared to have kids because I had a destabilizing childhood," I told her during our first session.

"You're onto something with that, my dear," she answered. "Go deeper with it and speak louder."

"When I was a kid . . ." I continued.

"Louder," she interrupted, tapping her ear with her index finger.

"When I was a kid, my parents moved from Argentina to the United States, then back to Argentina and, once again, back to the United States, all in the span of eight years," I yelled as loud as I could. It felt so cathartic that I briefly wondered if the key to healing was to scream your problems at someone.

Another thing about Betty was that her husband, Nestor, a man with an important, protruding stomach and incredibly skinny legs that looked like toothpicks, was an integral part of our sessions, as he was constantly walking into the room, forgetting that she was with a client. One time the man wandered in and Betty thought she muted the Zoom when she actually hadn't, and I heard her say something to him along the lines of "I'm in the middle of session with the failed child star." It was an interesting way to put it, "the failed child star," but she wasn't wrong; at age nine I gained some notoriety in Argentina for my sexual Madonna impersonations. I went on to get booked for a children's TV show, but had it suddenly taken away after my parents decided to move back to the United States.

Betty wasn't only Argentine; she was Argentine *and* Jewish, like me. I figured it meant that, culturally, she'd be acquainted with issues that are common in my family: the codependency, the lack of boundaries, the sexual openness that can sometimes be straight-up inappropriate. But, thinking back, I don't think Betty was familiar with the levels of odd shit my family is capable of. She was actually speechless when I told her that my family's favorite activity to do together was to get in my grandma's car and have her drive us to look at prostitutes in Buenos Aires's red-light district, or that my grandpa sold poppers for a living. Betty was confused as hell when I told her that my mom and dad can't do anything without each other being present, and that most of the jobs they've held have been a partnership: from opening a food court stand at a mall to driving catering trucks to operating my mom's OnlyFans page, where she shows pictures of her bunions and her bare ass and tits.

There's also the possibility that Betty was a disaster of a therapist. Perhaps Betty had nothing to do with me reaching the conclusion that I might want kids after all. I think what helped me get there was writing this book. It was this book that helped me to process that ping-pong of emotions I suffered as a child, caused by the constant moving back and forth from the United States to Argentina. It was this book that helped me reconcile with the fact that when I was a kid, everyone around me, including myself, was convinced that I'd become a big pop star one day, and that never actually happened. It was this book that made me come to terms with my unstable and dysfunctional upbringing that, until now, had me questioning if I'd be able to bring a child into this world and do things differently for them. The thing is, as I finished this book, I came to realize that all of these reasons that had deterred me from wanting to have kids were the exact same reasons I should have them. My unique and complicated life experiences made me adaptable. They made me wise. And I came out on top.

All of this clarity hit me during one of my final meetings with Betty. We were in the middle of a session when we both heard a loud bang, followed by the voice of her husband screaming something that I couldn't make out. "Is everything alright?" I asked her.

"My husband fell in the bathtub. I'll be right back," she said to me. She then got up and left me staring at my own reflection for about twenty minutes. At first, I was uncomfortable as fuck, sitting there, looking at my own face. I kind of wanted to die. And then something interesting happened. I started *really* looking at my own face, genuinely seeing myself. I smiled at myself, waved at myself in the camera, even blew myself a little kiss. "Tam, you're so cute," I thought. "Look how far you've come. How much better would the world be if there were more people like you running around?" I was feeling true love for myself for the first time in my life. That was the exact moment I decided I was going to try to do a motherhood. Anyways, enough of this having kids shit; that's not what this book is about. It's the story of everything that happened before I got there.

PART I

Argentina

A Bunch of Selfish
Pieces of Shit

I was born in Buenos Aires, Argentina. Everything on my end of the birth went smoothly. As a seven-pound fetus who knew absolutely nothing about the world, I did great. I was correctly positioned in my mother's womb. I didn't tear anything on my way out. I did my job. Everything that surrounded my birth, however, was a chaotic mess. That's because my family, those who were supposed to be the adults in the room, behaved like insane people. Especially my grandparents.

When I think about how my grandparents carried themselves on the day of my birth, I wholeheartedly understand why the rest of my life went down the way it did. It makes perfect sense that Mom and Dad would want to get the hell out of Argentina and immigrate to the United States in order to get as far as possible from them. Even if it meant starting over with nothing. It also makes sense that they would be convinced to return to Argentina.

The plan for my birth was as follows: My parents were going to have a calm, relaxed morning in their one-bedroom apartment, which was in a lower- to middle-class, predominantly Jewish neighborhood by the name of Villa Crespo. Villa Crespo is often referred to as Villa Kreplach (kreplach is a staple food in Ashkenazi cuisine, basically a Jewish wonton). Dad was going to make Mom breakfast in bed, and they'd slowly make their way over to the hospital, where my four grandparents were going to meet them and be present at the time of my birth.

My mom wasn't too keen on the fact that her mother, her father, *and* her in-laws were going to be standing in the delivery room, looking directly into her vagina as she pushed out a baby. She and my father had initially shut the idea down. They changed their minds, however, after my grandparents sat them down in what felt like an intervention and sprayed them with hoses of Jewish guilt. "How can you be so selfish as to keep us from witnessing the birth of our first grandchild?" cried Nilda, my paternal grandmother, a controlling, five-foot-one woman shaped like a dumpling, who sported a butch haircut and wore muumuus. My mom's parents agreed with Nilda. (This actually may have been the only time in their lives that they all agreed on anything.)

Mom and Dad stood their ground, however. None of them were to enter that delivery room, and that was the end of the conversation. Being left with no other choice, their parents went right for the jugular: "If you don't let us into that delivery room, we'll stop helping you with your rent and you'll have to move in with one of us." Mom and Dad gave each other a knowing glance full of despair and resignation. They knew they were fucked.

At the time, Dad was still attending the University of Buenos Aires, where he was studying architecture. When he wasn't in school, he worked odd jobs that didn't pay enough for the two of them to survive. Plus, the economy was in shambles and inflation was through the roof after a seven-year military dictatorship, which had just come to an end. The truth was, my parents were reliant on their parents for money. They were fucked indeed. "Fine," Dad answered, "all we ask of the four of you is that you behave like civilized adults, and that you don't make the day about you."

So, on the morning of November 22, 1983, when Mom felt her first contraction, Dad called all four of my grandparents on his rotary phone to tell them today was the day. "Meet us in the hospital in an hour," he said, reminding them to remain on their best behavior. A half hour later, as my parents were packing an overnight bag to take to the hospital, enjoying their last hour alone as a couple, there was a knock at the door. Guess who was standing outside? My grandparents, who entered the apartment with the force of the Tasmanian Devil. Four *Looney Tunes* characters, ready to wreak havoc upon my parents.

Nilda came into the apartment carrying what felt like one hundred bags that were overflowing with yarn. "I'm not finished with the sweater yet!" she announced to the room. This was a bad sign. That's because, for months leading up to my birth, Nilda had been hand-knitting my dad a beige and brown, chunky wool sweater that she was set on him wearing during my delivery. This sweater, which my mom now describes as being a color that resembled "diarrhea," was meant as a symbol of love from Nilda to her son. It was important for her that he wear it (even though it was a humid, eighty-degree day in which no one had any business wearing anything made of wool). My mom had become sick and tired of hearing about this fucking sweater. As a matter of fact, the simple sight of yarn had caused her to break out into hives while she was pregnant with me. (In the present day, Mom still refuses to wear wool, claiming that she's "developed an allergy to it.") That's because any time she brought up anything related to the pregnancy, her mother-in-law would interrupt her to talk about the garment's status—how close she was to finishing one of the sleeves, or how many inches from the bottom she was. My mom hated that thing. So when Nilda came in that day, announcing that she wasn't finished with the sweater yet and needed "forty minutes, give or take, to finish it," Mom literally fantasized about taking one of the knitting needles, stabbing my dad's mother in the neck, and killing her.

Pocho, my mother's father, walked into the apartment carrying something just as annoying as Nilda's bags of yarn, if not more: a two-foot long silver platter that was overflowing with salami, which he'd DOUSED with mustard. "It made our entire apartment stink like a butcher shop," recalls my father. It didn't matter that it was still ten in the morning, or that Mom had suffered from severe morning sickness her entire pregnancy whenever she smelled any type of meat. "It's salami time!" he exclaimed joyfully while placing this decadent tray of flesh on the dining table. "Today calls for a celebratory spread, and if anyone here doesn't eat a slice of salami, then you can go ahead and lick my hairy ass," he added.

Pocho was larger than life and intimidating as can be. He was six-three, boisterous and foul-mouthed, just like I am today. He looked and acted exactly like Rodney Dangerfield. It was no surprise to anyone that Pocho had come in carrying a tray full of cold cuts. The man had an abnormal obsession, almost a kink, with cured meats. He was known for hosting lavish soirees in which he'd make otherworldly charcuterie spreads. During these parties he'd spend all night standing by the table, monitoring which guests ate or didn't eat from his spreads. When someone refused to eat, he'd roast the shit out of them and never invite them over again. It was because of Pocho that I took my first bite of salami when I was just under a year old and almost choked to death. (I'm actually *almost* as obsessed with salami as Pocho. I've hosted a podcast by the name of *Chorizo Talk*, in which I try out a different kind of cured meat in each episode. I also recently got into a fight with a bouncer at a club because I happened to have two salamis inside my purse and he wouldn't let me enter with them and attempted, and failed, to confiscate them from me.)

Pocho's wife, my maternal grandmother Rita, a cold woman with coarse auburn hair and a bad facelift, entered the apartment with a Parisienne cigarette hanging out of her mouth. She continued to chain-smoke, indoors, for the remainder of the morning, disregarding the fact that her daughter was not only pregnant but also severely asthmatic. Rita had also chain-smoked the entire time she was pregnant with my mother. Rita was so addicted to nicotine that her doctor actually allowed her to light a cigarette while she was in the middle of delivering Mom.

Last but not least, there was Benjamín, my dad's dad. He was a Turkish Jew with old-school values. When *he* walked in that day, the first thing he said to Dad was "You better bless me with a boy." This wasn't the first time Benjamín had made a comment regarding my future sex. If I had to guess, I'd say his remarks were directly linked to why my parents didn't want the doctor to tell them whether I was a boy or a girl ahead of time. They simply assumed I'd be a boy and had already named me Jonathan. That's why, later that day, when they realized they'd birthed a girl, my parents had no idea what to name me. They asked the nurse to tell them what the couple in the adjacent room had named their newborn daughter. When she told them that the other parents had named their baby Tamara, my parents said, "Sounds good, let's name her that too."

Eventually, when Mom's contractions became more frequent, and Dad announced to the group that they really needed to head for the hospital, Nilda looked up at them and said, "I need five more minutes on this sweater. Maybe ten." None of my other grandparents seemed to find this request strange. As for my parents, they sat there like two schmucks, silently festering, until the sweater was fully finished.

The six adults then packed into my father's bright orange stick shift Ford Falcon and raced to the hospital. It was during this bumpy ride through the cobblestone streets of El Once, Buenos Aires's hectic garment district, that Mom's water broke, soaking the entire front seat. At that moment Mom snapped. She actually hated everyone in that car, including herself, for not being able to stand up to her parents. "I'm not gonna make it!" she screamed, turning around to look at my four grandparents, who were scrunched into the back seat.

"And it's all because of you. You're a bunch of selfish pieces of shit."

My four grandparents arrived at the hospital visibly offended at the fact that Mom had just called them all pieces of shit. Nevertheless, they sprinted down the hallway toward the delivery room, carrying their bags of yarn, their trays, and their cigarettes.

Even though Mom barely made it to the delivery room, everyone was present for my birth just as they'd hoped. My grandparents weren't in the room for long, however. Because the moment I came out, and the nurse held me up for everyone to see, they realized that their first grandchild was the ugliest baby that had ever been birthed: wrinkled like an old man's scrotum, with bushy eyebrows, hair in places there should be no hair (like my earlobes and my nose), and a body covered in eczema. I don't know what they were expecting me to look like. It's true that babies aren't known for being born looking perfect, but Dad said I looked like Abe Vigoda. I was so ugly that, one by one, my grandparents silently left the room, speechless. My misogynistic grandfather was so distracted by my ugliness he didn't even pay attention to the fact that I was born with a vagina.

The silver lining here is that, by being born ugly, I scared off my grandparents and gave my parents a moment of peace. From day one I was trying to protect them. As for the sweater, Dad did tell me that the moment Mom placed me in his arms for the first time, I became mesmerized by the beige and brown chunky wool, clutching the fabric in my tiny fists.

Pussy Fingers

Mom and Dad met when they were teenagers, and they're still together, more than fifty years later. They are codependent beyond words. Sometimes Mom cries when she goes to get her nails done or to Ross Dress for Less, because she doesn't like being separated from him for more than fifteen minutes. They're completely enmeshed with each other. One person with two heads, four arms, four legs, a penis, and a vagina. Always together.

My parents didn't meet in Buenos Aires, the city where I was born. They met in a remote, forgotten town with dirt roads by the name of Paso de los Libres, which sits right at the border of Argentina and Brazil.

They took me on vacation to Paso de los Libres when I was a kid, if you can call that a vacation. Even though I was younger than ten years old, that trip was the first time in my life I got a taste of what true depression felt like. The first thing I witnessed as we pulled up to town was a young woman walking on the side of the road, dazed and completely naked with her giant bush on display. We then drove straight to my dad's uncle's farm. Uncle Berat looked two hundred years old and was missing way too many teeth. He greeted me with a wet kiss that he planted way too close to my mouth, and there were chickens running around everywhere, pecking at my feet. One of his chickens ended up chasing me around the yard, trying to attack me. That day was so horrifying for me that I developed a lifelong fear of birds. (Since then, my relationship with birds has been dark. It's nearly impossible for me to sit outside at a restaurant and risk pigeons walking near my feet, especially if I'm wearing open-toed shoes. I rarely go to the beach because of the seagulls. And *if* I attend any picnics near lakes, I become a miserable human who spends the entire time looking around for approaching ducks. The fear is so irrational that, as I write this, in my office, inside my home, I felt the urge to look under my desk for potential birds.)

Before I get to why my parents ended up in Paso de los Libres, I want to give you a little background about my grandparents.

Benjamín, my paternal grandfather, was the son of Turkish immigrants who moved to Argentina in the early 1900s along with millions of other immigrants who were trying to get in on the country's quickly growing economy. They picked Buenos Aires not only because it was the capital but because it was known as the "Paris of South America." After settling, my great-grandparents made a fortune selling fabric and doing some other mafia-esque things that I can never get a straight answer about.

My grandfather, a man with a face full of pockmarks caused by smallpox, and a whole lot of swagger, married my grandma Nilda when they were just seventeen. She didn't come from a wealthy family like he did. She was the daughter of poor Jewish communists who fled a pogrom in Poland during the early 1900s and traveled through Europe having babies in every country along the way, which is why my grandma has siblings with creative nicknames such as "The Dutch," "The French," "The Austrian," and "The Portuguese." They eventually ended up in Argentina, where Nilda, their youngest, was born. My great-grandparents and their nine children lived in a one-bedroom apartment. They never learned Spanish and spoke only Yiddish, using their children as translators.

Because the family was so poor, Nilda never went to school, and she didn't learn to read and write until she was an adult. At only thirteen years old, she started working as a cook at a brothel where her aunt worked as a prostitute. The women working the brothel were mostly Jewish immigrants who taught Nilda how to replicate the Jewish cuisine of their motherland, which they were deeply nostalgic for. So, at a very early age, Nilda was cooking Ashkenazi dishes from eastern Europe as well as Sephardic dishes from the Middle East.

As a matter of fact, some of my earliest memories are of Nilda's cooking. During my early childhood we'd gather every Saturday at her apartment, which overlooked Calle Corrientes, one of Buenos Aires's busiest and loudest streets, and she'd prepare for the entire family what she referred to as a "light lunch." Her definition of a light lunch was a table with no less than twenty dishes that she'd spent more than a day preparing. Dishes from chicken liver to Gefilte fish to peppers stuffed with rice. She shoved so much food down your gullet that you felt like you were going to explode. It wasn't uncommon to see people unbuckling their pants, sweating, and falling asleep halfway through the meal. One of Nilda's brothers tried to play tennis after eating one of her "light lunches," and died of a heart attack.

Nilda and Benjamín met because of her cooking. This happened after my grandfather paid a visit to his favorite brothel and was offered a taste of one of Nilda's boyoz, Sephardic pastries that she'd made by hand. He was so blown away by this dish that he asked to meet the cook, and they were married a few weeks later.

Benjamín expected his new wife to be nothing but grateful and submissive, as he'd just rescued her from poverty. But she wasn't. She turned out to be a total maniac who did whatever needed to be done in order to feel in control of her life. During their honeymoon, Benjamín spent all day gambling at the casino, leaving Nilda alone in their hotel room. When she demanded that he give her attention, he dismissed her, so one night, Benjamín came home from the casino and found that she had taken his razor and shaved off an entire patch of hair at the top of her head, in the shape of a circle. When grandpa saw his new half-bald bride, looking like a Capuchin friar, and asked her what the fuck she'd done, Nilda answered, "This is what you're going to have to look at now. If you keep gambling, I'll shave the rest of it off." He never gambled again.

As for my mom's parents, I know a little less about their history. Mostly because everyone on their side of the family is either dead or hates each other. In fact, a few years ago, I tried emailing one of Pocho's only remaining family members, a cousin who's in his nineties and lives in Italy. Over email I asked him if he could provide me with any information regarding Pocho's youth, and he basically told me to go fuck myself. "Dear Tamara," he replied, "I will not give you any information about your grandfather. That's because I couldn't care less about the past. I'm only interested in the future." What a little bitch. What future could this ninety-year-old have!? It made me so mad. I couldn't help myself and replied to the email with a GIF of a nude, succulent Shrek bending over and blowing kisses with his butthole.

The few things I do know about Pocho was that, as a teenager, he was drafted into the Argentine army. He was eventually dishonorably discharged after he contracted crabs and got caught picking the lice from his pubes and scattering them on the food of his superiors. After getting kicked out of the army, he spent a few years in jail for a crime that was never talked about during my youth, and then became a trumpet player and an orchestra conductor. One night, a very wealthy Jewish businessman hired my grandpa's orchestra to play at his daughter's sixteenth birthday party. The man's daughter turned out to be my grandmother, Rita.

Some people have told me that Rita was stunning in her youth. That she resembled a young Elizabeth Taylor and was crowned Miss Jewish Buenos Aires several years in a row. I've also heard that Rita's father, my great-grandpa, paid to have those pageants rigged for his daughter to win. Nevertheless, Rita was a spoiled socialite who hung around Eva Perón and her sisters, giving away food and sewing machines to poor people while drinking champagne. Rita was a lush who didn't want to settle down with a nice, boring Jewish boy, she wanted a bad boy. Someone who was an ex-convict, who drank, and played the trumpet, and had genital lice. Someone just like Pocho.

Fast-forward to the 1960s, when both of my grandfathers got word that there was a small border town by the name of Paso de los Libres where business was booming. Turns out Brazilians were crossing the border by the dozens, desperate to spend their money and take advantage of Argentina's cheap prices, caused by their weak currency. My grandfathers, who by now had become merchants and were starting to blow through whatever money their parents had left them, saw this as an opportunity for economic growth. So they packed up their families and their belongings and left Buenos Aires.

In Paso de los Libres, each family opened up a store. Benjamín's store sold women's clothing. Pocho's store, on the other hand, sold records and poppers. Yes, *those* poppers. People used to flock to his store by the hundreds so that they could buy these little jars which grandpa filled with his own hands. Mom remembers that people would put the little jars up to their nose, take a sniff, and act like idiots for a few seconds. A few years ago, I brought a bottle of poppers to a pool party that my parents threw at their house. After some convincing, I got my mom to sniff it, and the two of us got high as shit. "My dad was onto something," Mom said to me with a giant smile plastered on her face while she danced to Cher's "Believe" wearing nothing but a thong.

At first, maintaining a social life was tough in this new town. One of the few things it had to offer was that, once a year, it hosted its own sadder version of Brazil's Carnaval, utilizing smaller floats, fewer feathers, and worse dancers. Also, unlike Buenos Aires, which had one of the largest and most tight-knit Jewish populations in Latin America, Paso de los

Libres was home to only two Jewish couples: Benjamín and Nilda and Pocho and Rita. I wish I could say that, upon meeting, the two couples became the best of friends, but that wasn't the case. The truth was, they couldn't really stand each other. Despite this, they still hung out every weekend because they were all Jewish. It also just so happened that they had a son and a daughter who were close in age.

When Mom met Dad, she didn't know what kissing was. She was a naive fourteen-year-old girl with no curves who still played with dolls, and still hadn't gotten her period. She was fearful of the world around her and suffered from a debilitating shyness. Part of the reason for her reclusive nature was that her older sister, Sandra, required all of my grandparents' attention, leaving Mom somewhat neglected.

My aunt Sandra's life was difficult from birth. She was delivered using forceps, which severely damaged her right arm, rendering it somewhat immobile for the remainder of her life. When she was a teenager, a doctor discovered that she had fibroids in her uterus, and instead of removing them, he decided to perform a full-on hysterectomy without her really understanding what it meant. Sandra was also schizophrenic and never properly treated for it. She'd go through bouts of paranoia and delusion where she was convinced that she was friends with presidents, and she was always talking about the various doctorate degrees she held in fields like sociology and marine biology, none of which were real. (When Mom was pregnant with me, Sandra had one of her scariest psychotic episodes, claiming that people were out to get her, and that someone was placing shards of glass in her food and inside her shoes.)

Add the fact that my grandparents were socialites who were all about appearances and fun times, and lacked any understanding about mental illness, and you have yourself a recipe for disaster. Meanwhile, Mom sort of dissociated from all the chaos that went on in the household by staying in her room and pretending like she was still a child, playing with her toys until she was fourteen. She was slightly feral, like a weird version of Jodie Foster in *Nell*. *Chicka, chicka, chickabee.*

When Mom saw Dad for the first time, she fell so in love she froze. She actually just stood there, staring at him, completely transfixed until she started drooling. He was a sixteen-year-old playboy who drove a light-blue Fiat 128, wore polyester bell bottoms with platform shoes, and would spend hours in front of the mirror, blow-drying his hair with a round brush. He was obsessed with his hair, and not just the hair on his head. Dad cared so much about his appearance that after a shower, he'd prop up one of his legs on the sink and use the same round brush to blow-dry his pubes. He still blow-dries his pubes, but he claims that *now* "it's not for looks, it's for hygienic reasons."

At first, Dad barely noticed Mom. As a matter of fact, he was dating an older Brazilian woman at the time who he claimed had one perky breast and another breast that was deflated and sagged down to her waist, which was caused by her being hit with a baseball bat across the chest. Nevertheless, Mom was so obsessed with Dad that she cried every day because he didn't even notice her. Such was her obsession that, on her fifteenth birthday, her mother gifted her a bottle of the same cologne my dad wore so that she could smell him. Grandma also gifted Mom with a visit to see a Brazilian witch whom she used to frequent whenever she wanted to put evil spells on people she hated.

Aside from putting evil spells on people, this witch was known to cure illnesses, put an end to love troubles, or predict your future. Mom and Rita crossed the border into Brazil, and when they arrived at this witch's house, they were greeted by a woman dressed all in white, smoking a cigar and chugging whiskey out of a bottle. "What is the problem with your child?" she asked Rita, who listed a few of the things she was hoping to accomplish during that visit.

"She's in love with someone who doesn't notice her. She just turned fifteen and still hasn't gotten her period, and she has no breasts," Rita answered. "Can you fix it?"

The witch took my mom into an adjacent room, made her lie down naked in a bathtub, and drenched her in goat's blood while she chanted something in Portuguese. After this terrifying experience, she returned Mom to Rita. "That should do it," the woman said. "You'll notice a change in a matter of days."

As promised, a week later, Mom was sitting in her room, brushing her doll's hair, when she got a stomachache so intense that she felt like she was being split into two. She'd gotten her period. She also began noticing that her chest started to expand. A few weeks later, she had tits the size of two large watermelons.

It wasn't just her body that was changing; Mom began to move around the world with a confidence that left her unrecognizable. She also developed a passion for music and dancing, similar to the one I would possess as a preteen. If there was music playing, Mom was dancing. And she danced well. She was especially good at samba dancing. (Today, in her mid-sixties, Mom still dances with a stamina that I truly cannot comprehend. She can dance until two in the morning if my dad doesn't wrangle her.) No one understood how she learned how to samba dance or where it came from. Her love of music had been inside her all along, and she passed it down to me. That same year, during Carnaval, my mom was standing on the sidelines, watching the colorful floats go by, when she turned to her parents and said, "I'm going in." She then took off her clothes and shoes and joined the parade. She danced down Paso de los Libres's dirt roads, barefoot, with nothing but a bra and underwear on, as her big naturals flopped up and down. At the end of the night, she was crowned "Queen of Carnaval."

A little while later, after Dad returned from spending a few months in Buenos Aires, all four of my grandparents went on vacation to the beach with their teenage children. While my dad was lying face up on a towel, tanning, my newly developed mother approached him. She stood there, towering over him, completely blocking the sun. When he looked up at her, he saw a woman so spectacularly beautiful, with "breasts as large as two human heads," as he puts it, that he got an instant erection, so noticeable that, in order to hide it, he was forced to spend the next couple of hours lying face down.

When they returned from that vacation, my dad broke up with his Brazilian girlfriend and asked Mom out on their first date. At the end of the night, he returned her to her parents' house, where Pocho happened to be throwing a party. Pocho felt resentful toward Dad for ignoring his daughter all those years and making her suffer, so he asked Dad to come in. He told Mom to wait in her room so as to not embarrass her, then turned to Dad and said, "Let me smell your fingers." Dad knew what was coming next. Pocho took a big whiff off Dad's index finger. "They smell like pussy!" Pocho announced to the crowd. "Welcome to the family," he added. He then raised his glass and made the entire party toast.

"To my future son-in-law, Pussy Fingers."

"To Pussy Fingers!" the crowd replied in total merriment.

My parents got the hell out of Paso de los Libres as soon as they could, only to be followed back to Buenos Aires by their parents. They were married shortly after Mom turned eighteen.

The Pink Balloon

In the months after my birth I transformed from an uggo fuggo baby into what my parents describe as a living doll. Just like Mom, who shed her sheepish demeanor and emerged a dancing queen with a pair of unforgettable massive milkers, I too shed my eczema, body hair, and all-around rodentness and turned into a cherubic baby with rosy cheeks, and eyes so big and green that people would stop my parents on the street just to get a good look.

The fact that I was my grandparents' first grandchild, *and* the first kid to be born within my parents' large group of friends, caused me to get an unhealthy amount of attention. A smothering, if you will. Our apartment had a constant flow of people coming in and out who were desperate to munch on my folds, watch me get my ass wiped, and hear me say goo-goo-gah-gah. It didn't matter what time it was. Dad, for example, would finish class around nine P.M. and come home with a few of his friends from school who wanted to see me. They disregarded the fact that Mom had struggled for hours to get me to fall asleep. They'd just wake me right up to make funny faces at me. There were no boundaries and no schedule.

For the first years of my life, I was showered with endless toys, lavish amounts of attention, and no opportunity to learn what self-soothing was. And then, a few months after I turned four, my little sister was born. She was an adorable jelly bean who was constantly laughing. Everyone was obsessed with her, and in the space of a day, I went from excessive attention to *nothing.* So I started biting people.

The first time I bit someone, I was four and a half. It was Dad, and he had to get six stitches on his hand because I tore through the flesh. During pre-K I attached my mouth to a little boy's cheek like a rabid dog, furiously biting into it and refusing to let go. That summer, I crawled up to one of my grandparents' friends who had fallen asleep on a beach chair, wearing a Speedo, and I bit right into his ball sack. He screamed so loud you could hear it from across the ocean. The man had to be rushed to the hospital.

The act of me biting someone's nuts was concerning enough that my parents sent me to a child psychologist. My first. Psychoanalysis is huge in Argentina, especially in Buenos Aires. As a matter of fact, in 2005, Argentina was ranked as a world leader in psychologists per capita. During my sessions, my therapist would give me playdough and tell me to displace my anger on the dough in hopes of getting me to stop attacking people with my teeth. Instead of pounding and squeezing the dough, however, I'd put it in my mouth and bite the shit out of it, my eyes rolling to the back of my head from the pleasurable feeling of destroying something with my teeth.

And then, when I turned five, my favoritest grandpa of all, Pocho, decided to take matters into his own hands and give me an evening that would make me feel like the most special girl in the world. One Saturday, he picked me up from my parents' apartment and told me he'd gotten tickets to see a play in Buenos Aires's theater district. It was a live-action *My Little Pony* musical. And they weren't just any tickets, they were VIP, all-access passes that would allow me to go backstage and meet and greet the ponies themselves.

The reason Pocho was able to acquire these bad boys was that, in the early eighties, he'd made enough money selling poppers that he'd purchased the rights to *My Little Pony*, in Argentina. What a career shift! This authorized him to manufacture backpacks, clothing, binders, and pretty much whatever he wanted and stamp images of *My Little Pony* characters and logos on them without getting sued.

It was my first time at the theater, and everything about the experience blew my little mind. But there were two things I specifically recall. One was the elation I felt when the theater's lights dimmed, as the show was about to start. Those ten seconds felt like a sacred moment in which real life faded away and a new dream world of magic and play appeared. I wanted to live in that moment forever. The second thing I remember was wanting to rush the stage and join the dancers. I didn't belong with the audience, I belonged up there, singing and dancing with the ponies. Little did I know that six years later I would be performing in a nearby theater.

After the show, Pocho tied a pink *My Little Pony* balloon around my little wrist, which would commemorate my special night. He then took me backstage where I got to meet all the ponies (which were actually just two grown men inside a horse costume). But I didn't care. I felt like a celebrity, posing for pictures with them, shaking their "hands," and petting their rainbow hair. Not only did I feel like a special princess with my pink balloon, but I had also discovered the theater. I had a new obsession. And suddenly, my desire to bite had completely left my body.

When Pocho and I exited the theater, the balloon suddenly loosened from my wrist and floated up into the sky. Pocho and I stood there in silence for a while, holding hands, watching that pink balloon go up, up, up, until it turned into a dot.

I didn't feel sadness or anger about the loss of the balloon. I felt a new kind of sensation running through my body. It was as if, by losing that balloon, I was also losing the perfect night with my grandpa. Like something belonged to me for a brief time, and just as I was starting to enjoy it, I'd lost it. This feeling would come to define my life: nostalgia.

That night, I slept over at my grandpa and grandma's apartment. Going forward, Saturday night sleepovers at Pocho and Rita's house would end up becoming a ritual for me. The best night of the week. I would lie in bed, snuggled between them, eating from a tray of neatly sliced fruit, which they referred to as a "Fruit Party." After I fell asleep, Pocho would move me to the spare bedroom, and the two of them would watch TV shows like *Porcel Y Sus Gatitas*, which translates to "Porcel and His Pussies." This was an iconic 1980s Argentine variety show in which the host, El Gordo Porcel, a comedian who weighed about six hundred pounds, inappropriately touched his half-naked background dancers, who were dressed like kittens from the musical *Cats*. Make a note for yourself to look up "Gatitas de Porcel" on YouTube. The show's opening dance routine is one of the horniest and most excellent things I've ever seen in my life.

The next morning, when I woke up and walked into their bedroom, Pocho was listening to the radio very attentively. "You won't believe what happened," he said to me. "I just heard a report on the radio. A girl your age, named Tamara, with brown hair and green eyes, just like you, but who lives in the United States of America and speaks English, was playing in her garden this morning when a pink *My Little Pony* balloon descended from the sky. The girl grabbed the balloon and called her local radio station to report that she had found it, so they gave her free tickets to see the U.S. production of the *My Little Pony* musical. Your balloon floated to the United States, and someone just like you found it and is getting to do exactly what you did!"

I was quite a spoiled child, so you'd think I'd be jealous over the fact that some other girl ended up with something of mine. But I felt nothing but joy. I was so happy for this other Tamara, who looked just like me and spoke English, to get to experience what I did. I wondered if her grandfather would be taking her to the show, just like mine did. I wondered if she'd get to go backstage like me, and if she'd try to shake the pony's nonexistent hand. I wondered if I'd ever meet her.

As I write this, I'm crying my ass off thinking of what an amazing grandfather Pocho was. I miss him so much. How lucky was I to have him? It also dawns on me that there's a whole other layer to this balloon story. Who was this other Tamara who lived in the United States? Pocho didn't know that, not long after this, my parents would be packing up all of our belongings and moving us to the United States. My parents didn't even know they'd be doing it yet. Was this other Tamara living in the United States a ghost ship of me? Or was the Argentine Tamara a ghost ship of hers?

Jacaranda Trees

In November 1989, right after I turned six, Dad took me to see Buenos Aires's famous jacarandas. It was spring, and the recently bloomed trees had turned the city a peaceful shade of lavender blue, which gave the streets a dreamlike quality. "I have something to tell you," Dad said, ripping off a handful of the jacaranda's flowers, then dropping them in my hand so that I could get a better look. "You, me, Mom, and your sister are moving to the United States."

I didn't understand what any of that meant. The information was too amorphous for me to process. He should have given me something more concrete to hold on to. For example, he could have said: "You, me, Mom, and your sister are moving to the same country as Mickey Mouse," or "We're moving to the country where Disneyland is." Anything Walt Disney related would have done the trick. (If you ever decide to immigrate to the United States and want to break the news to your small child, just tell them Disneyland will be a part of their future. Tell them Donald Duck and Goofy will be coming over for dinner every night. Lie to them. It'll really help them out.)

"Why?" I asked.

"Well . . ." Dad answered. He hadn't expected this very simple follow-up question from me. "Because we're going to have a better life there," he said.

"But why?" I prodded.

Why? was a really good question. A question that I'm just now starting to understand as an adult, and as a result of writing this book. It wasn't only because we didn't have money and the Argentine economy was a disaster. Although all of that *is* true.

In fact, after I was born, Dad got his architecture degree and got a job at the Ministry of Public Works, where he didn't earn a single penny. At the end of every month, he would inquire about where his paycheck was, and they'd brush him off by telling him that "it was on the way." After six months of working there, the paycheck that was "on the way" finally arrived. When he went to deposit it at the bank, the teller told him the check had bounced. That was Dad's last day working as an architect.

Dad looked for alternatives, but jobs seemed scarce all around. He wasn't the only one having a hard time finding work. The majority of my parents' friends found themselves in similar situations. The only ones who seemed to get by were those who ended up working for their parents' already existing businesses, or those who came up with some sort of scam. Like their friend Lucho, a shady-ass, quack doctor who promised his patients he had a new, cutting-edge device that was guaranteed to help them lose weight. He then went out and bought a straight-up desk lamp, which he'd rub all over his patients' stomachs. "I've never looked better," they'd tell him after two or three sessions. Maybe he was onto something.

Finding no alternatives, Dad started working for Pocho, helping him design backpacks and raincoats, which Pocho would then stamp with *My Little Pony* logos. Sure, I loved my grandpa, but I have to imagine that working for him wasn't easy in the least bit; he was bossy and condescending, and still referred to my dad as "Pussy Fingers" more than five years later. Not only did Dad hate him, he was Pocho's bitch now.

Plus, it wasn't like Pocho's business was thriving. Even though democracy had returned in 1983, the country's wealth didn't. The government was printing and borrowing money like crazy to keep up with its enormous spending, which caused levels of hyperinflation that people couldn't keep up with. I'm going to make up a new form of currency to give you an example (because I understand shit like this only when it's explained to me like I'm a child). Let's say Pocho's company would spend thirty Argentine dingledoos to manufacture a backpack, but by the time the product was finished and ready to be sold, that backpack was now only worth ten dingledoos. Another example: My sister's diapers may have cost something like five dingledoos in the morning, and at night the price would skyrocket to thirty. It drove people crazy, and there was no keeping up with the value of things.

My parents had also become exhausted from the city's constant flooding and power outages. Their car got broken into multiple times, and Dad had gotten robbed at gunpoint once and pickpocketed twice. Add to that the never-ending manipulation and guilt coming from my insufferable grandparents who felt that they had a right to criticize and interfere with every single decision their children made, and you have yourself an answer to my Why?

But why the United States? The answer is simple. For one, my grandparents didn't live there. Also, Mom and Dad had honeymooned in the United States, and they found that the roads were always clean, the prices were reasonable, and "people were always smiling."

A few months after Dad took me to see the jacaranda trees, our apartment was completely empty except for a few items they weren't able to sell, like Mom's rocking chair, where Pocho sat, silently weeping, coming up with a plan. There was also the refrigerator, which Nilda had purchased from us. She didn't need it, but it was her way of helping us out without admitting that she was helping us out. Every bone in that woman's body wanted us to stay in Argentina. Despite this, she'd showed up at our place early in the morning wearing a velour tracksuit and carrying two dozen pastries, but she refused to say a single word or make eye contact with anyone.

The apartment was filled with uncles, aunts, friends, and cousins who came to say goodbye, and there was a somber energy in the air, reminiscent of a funeral. My sister and I still didn't understand what was happening. We were in our own world, taking a last Argentine bath while conducting experiments. I had mixed shampoo, conditioner, bobby pins, Coca-Cola, and mayonnaise, which I acquired from the nearly empty refrigerator earlier that day when no one was looking. "Take a sip if you want to be strong like Mr. T," I said to my sister, who obeyed and went on to barf all over the tub. As the two of us sat there, covered in vomit water, Mom walked into the bathroom holding a towel.

"It's time to go to the airport," she said.

PART II

The United States

Rabbits in My Throat

Mom was only twenty-six when she boarded a nineteen-hour Aerolíneas Argentinas flight that would take her, me, and my sister from Buenos Aires to Los Angeles, California. Dad had flown to the United States a few months before us, in hopes of finding a job and a place for us to live.

Dad tried his luck in Miami first. He picked this city specifically because Nilda's best friend from youth (a woman who'd been cruelly nicknamed "Baldy" because she'd suffered from postmenopausal balding and had only a few strands of hair left on her head, which she'd tease the shit out of and then cover in super-hold hairspray in order to make it appear fuller) gave Dad the phone number of a guy she knew in Miami who'd probably be willing to help us settle there. (Nilda ended up giving Baldy the silent treatment for years because she felt that her best friend had betrayed her by helping her son move to another country.)

The contact Dad was given was that of a man who'd left Argentina during the dictatorship and had been living in Miami for more than ten years. There, he'd become rich selling television sets. "I hear he's a saint," Baldy told Dad. "He hires every Argentine that's new in town and sponsors their work permit. He's the Mother Teresa of Argentine immigrants." When Dad landed in Miami and called the phone number he'd been given, he was utterly shocked when this "Mother Teresa of Argentine immigrants" told him to "eat shit and go back to rot in Argentina." (Dad didn't know that weeks before this phone call, the man had gotten five thousand dollars' worth of television sets stolen by one of the many Argentines he'd employed. So, from that day on, he decided he was done helping Argentines and became an anti-immigration, right-wing fanatic. Oh well.)

My father's second and only other contact in the United States was a guy in his twenties named Fernando. Mom attended group therapy sessions with Fernando, and on his last session, he informed the group that he was leaving Argentina to start a new life in Los Angeles (his reason for attending therapy was that he was a people pleaser, and it was ruining his life). It was a long shot, but Dad called Fernando to see if he could help him out. "Come stay with me. I can get you a job delivering newspapers," he told Dad without skipping a beat, leaving him speechless at the kindness of this stranger. If you ask me, his kindness could have ended there. Fernando, who clearly didn't learn much from his group therapy sessions, and remained a chronic people pleaser, kept going: "You can also take my bed. I'll sleep on the sofa." So, thanks to him, Los Angeles was to become our new home.

Shortly after, Dad gave Mom the green light to come meet him, and she got on that plane with two oversize suitcases, two small children, and a new perm that aged her about forty years. I had just turned six, but I remember every second of this plane ride.

The moment we took off, my sister started acting fussy (we later found out that she had a severe ear infection). This fussiness quickly devolved into an unbearable, high-pitched fit of crying that echoed throughout the entire cabin and was probably even audible in the sky. Five hours later, my sister hadn't stopped and was beginning to turn a shade of red that resembled raw meat. Mom was freaking out. She asked the flight attendants for help, telling them that she thought her baby was dying, but they seemed annoyed at the hysterical infant and simply suggested that Mom "put a pacifier in her mouth." The crying was so annoying that some man got out of his seat, walked up to us, and told Mom that if she didn't shut her baby up, he'd open the plane's emergency exit and push the three of us out.

Mom, who was having a full-blown panic attack, grabbed my hand so tightly that her pointy fingernails were digging into my flesh. I was fucking terrified. My sister was dying. My mom was crying. I didn't know where the hell I was going. And now a man was threatening to throw us out of the plane! On top of that, on the way to the airport, Pocho had given me a bag of salami slices and told me that if I ate it all, he'd come visit me soon, so I inhaled those round cold cuts as fast as I could even though I knew they always upset my stomach. Point being that the meats I'd eaten as the plane took off had disturbed my stomach in a bad way and were making me want to go poo like crazy. Now was not the time to ask Mom to take me to the bathroom, so I held it and sat there in agony. I wanted to cry too. But there was way too much going on, and the last thing I wanted to do was take up more space. Instead, I sat there with a huge knot in my throat, which I pushed down because I knew that if I cried, I'd just give Mom another thing to worry about.

These knots in my throat, caused by suppressing tears in order to not give my parents more preoccupations, started occurring very frequently after this experience. As a matter of fact, once we arrived in the States, I developed a nervous tic that would cause me to feel the need to clear my throat three or four times per minute because it felt like there was something furry, like a rabbit, stuck inside it. I called them the "rabbits in my throat." (It's crazy, but, later in life, I'd fall in love with writing after reading a short story by Julio Cortázar, one of the best Argentine writers of all time, titled "Letter to a Young Lady in Paris," in which the main character feels a similar tickle in his throat and goes on to vomit hundreds of rabbits.)

When we landed at LAX, I guarded the giant cart that held our suitcases and the stroller where my sister slept with a pacifier in her mouth while Mom nervously presented our passports to a United States immigration officer.

Outside the terminal, we were reunited with Dad, who gave Mom a passionate, tongue-filled kiss and lifted me and my sister up in his arms. It had been more than three months since we'd seen him.

"How was the flight?" he asked me.

"It was great!" I answered, even though it wasn't.

"Look what I bought," he said to me, pointing to an old Ford Taurus that he'd purchased for five hundred dollars, which he'd nicknamed "Semen" because of its creamy, off-white color. The trunk was broken and would pop open at random times while we were driving and scare the shit out of us, but I thought it was the coolest thing I'd ever seen.

Another thing about Semen was that it was missing the front bumper. The reason for this was that Dad had just come from driving all night while delivering newspapers. During the shift, Dad had fallen asleep behind the wheel and awoken to what he thought was the sound of fireworks but was actually just the bang of his car crashing into the side of the Hollywood Hills. As we drove away from the airport, Dad described the crash to Mom, explaining that he was able to complete the delivery route without falling asleep a second time by implementing a technique his uncle had once taught him, namely, to pinch his balls with his thumb and index fingers as hard as he could in order to stay awake. I sat in the back seat, looking out the window onto my new home, a sprawling land full of palm trees, freeways, and smog, while "Rick Dees in the Morning" blabbed away on 102.7 KIIS FM, in a language that I didn't yet understand.

After that ride, during which I saw more cars in fifteen minutes than I'd ever seen in my entire life, Dad exited the freeway and we pulled into a two-story, L-shaped building off the Sunset Strip. "Is this our house?" I asked Dad.

"That's right," he answered. "It's kind of our house. It's more like a hotel, except it starts with the letter M. A motel!" (Fernando had offered to let all of us stay at his one-bedroom apartment, but Dad turned him down, feeling like he'd be taking advantage of this man's kindness.)

The motel was . . . you know . . . really fucking bad. My sister and I were the only kids there. It stunk like cigarettes and old blood, and most of the guests were sex workers who rented the rooms by the hour. When we walked into our room, Mom instantly started crying. Dad told my sister and me to console her, and the four of us stood there hugging for a while. When her crying subsided, she began inspecting the room in great detail, running her fingers across the top of the dresser and the TV to see how dusty they were, smelling the towels, and inspecting the bed linens. "The towels smell like mold, and there's a few hairs on the pillowcases," she said to Dad before sending him off to buy us new sheets and towels. She also told us not to walk around with our shoes off, 'cause we'd catch a fungus on our toes.

Our first night in the United States, I stood on the bed and performed my favorite song from the *My Little Pony* musical for Mom because I knew that when I sang it for her, it always made her happy. Mom seemed to forget we were in a motel. She was smiling and clapping along with me and even told me that one day I was going to be a famous singer because she could tell that I "sang from the heart." This encouragement led me to sing the same song about fourteen more times, until Dad had to beg me to stop.

The four of us then laid in our full-size motel room bed together and watched *Harry and the Hendersons*. Even though I didn't understand what anyone in the movie was saying, I could tell that the bigfoot creature and I were going through something similar; we were both living in unfamiliar territory, surrounded by unfamiliar people. But regardless of what me and that hairy, armoire-size beast had in common, he still scared the living shit out of me. That night, I was awoken at two in the morning by strange noises coming from inside our motel room bathroom and realized that neither of my parents were in bed. I was paralyzed by fear, yet I managed to walk over to the bathroom door. Inside, I could hear Mom and Dad grunting and moaning. I thought Bigfoot was murdering my parents! I started screaming for help so loudly that I probably woke up every single occupant of that motel. Mom and Dad, who were obviously just a-suckin' and a-fuckin' in that bathroom, came out of there instantly and put me back in bed, reassuring me that there was no Bigfoot in the bathroom with them.

During my first few weeks in the United States, my favorite thing to do was to accompany Dad to work. He'd gotten a second job as a courier, picking up money from various businesses and then dropping it off for them at the bank. I loved going to work with Dad because staying at the motel with Mom was boring. Dad and I would drive through Beverly Hills, where I got to see people who looked like movie stars and cars that looked like spaceships. While Dad drove, I fed him carrots so that he wouldn't fall asleep, and he'd tell me about this amazing place we were going to move to soon. It was called "The San Fernando Valley," and it was a place where all the Argentines who moved to Los Angeles lived, and where I'd start school and make new friends. "What is a valley?" I asked Dad on one of these drives.

"It's a chunk of land between two mountains," he told me. He then pulled over and drew a picture of a hot dog on a napkin for me so that I could picture it better. "Look. This hot dog is kind of like a valley," he said. "The buns are the mountains, and the wiener is the valley part where we're going to live." This description made me even more confused than

I was before, but it didn't matter. I wanted to live in the glorious Valley. He even said that in the Valley there was a special supermarket for Argentines that sold all my favorite candy from Argentina. Every night, I helped Dad count the money he'd earned, knowing that the more money we had, the closer we'd be to living in the Valley.

As for Mom, being in the States was turning out to be harder than she'd imagined. Even though immigrating had been her idea in the first place, living in a motel was sending her into an emotional tailspin of depression, and whenever she exited the motel, she was completely filled with fear. For the most part, there was lots of crying and low moments. But it was around this time that I witnessed her mental unwellness manifest itself in rage form for the first time in my life. It happened three weeks after we'd been living in the U.S. Mom took my sister and me to a McDonald's that was down the street from the motel. I ordered a Happy Meal that came with a plastic chicken McNugget that had a face on it. My first toy in the United States of America! I was skipping around that McDonald's, waving my new little prize possession in the air, when I realized that Mom had started arguing with the cashier. I had no idea what the hell was happening, but Mom looked possessed. She began yelling at the cashier and became so unhinged that she grabbed a soda from our tray and chucked it at him, completely drenching him as well as all the bills in the register. Everything was dripping wet, and everyone was looking at us. I quickly stopped skipping and slipped the chicken nugget in my pocket as a security guard walked up to us and escorted Mom, my sister, and me out of the McDonald's. A horrifying situation. As we walked back to our motel room, I asked Mom why she was fighting with the cashier. "He gave me less change than he was supposed to," she said. "And he called us Latin trash," she added. I didn't know if being Latin trash was a good thing or bad thing, but I was going to assume, because of how the situation ended, that it was a bad thing.

That evening, when Dad got back from work, Mom told him about the fight she'd gotten into. Dad, who was in an extra good mood, told her things were going to get better very soon and that he had two really great bits of news for us. The first was that tonight was Halloween, a holiday that didn't exist in Argentina, where people got to dress up as anything they wanted to. He took us to a store called Thrifty's, where he bought Mom ice cream to cheer her up and told me I could pick out costumes for all of us to wear on Halloween. "We can't spend too much money," he said to me. "So get creative with our costumes." And then, as we were walking through the cleaning supply section, I got an idea.

"Let's dress up as trash bags," I said, remembering that the cashier had called us Latin trash earlier. Mom didn't love the idea, but Dad thought it was creative and affordable, so he bought a pack of extra-large, black trash bags, cut two holes for our arms to go in, and two holes for our legs to go in, and we each put the trash bags on like they were dresses. He even made a mini trash bag for my sister. We then walked around the crowded streets of West Hollywood during the yearly Halloween parade. There were drag queens everywhere, and they kept throwing candy at us and asking to take pictures with us. Our costumes were an absolute hit: a family of trash bags.

Dad delivered the second bit of good news later that night. After walking around the West Hollywood parade, he told us to get into the car and drove us up to Mulholland Drive. When we got to the top of the hill, he parked the car and turned off the headlights. That's when I saw it for the first time. It was so beautiful, with a million lights twinkling below us. "That's the San Fernando Valley," Dad told us. He then pulled out the keys to what was going to be our new apartment. "One of those little lights you see down there is our new home." All of a sudden, the terrible plane ride, the Bigfoot attack, and the horrifying McDonald's incident from earlier that day didn't matter anymore. Mom and Dad made out with tongues again, and then we drove back down the mountain and went straight to the motel to pack our bags.

I Get Some Beautiful Friends

The San Fernando Valley turned out to be a lot more pictur-esque when seen from above than experienced on the ground, and that's because it was 102 degrees the day we moved into our new apartment in Northridge. Our shoes felt like they were melting onto the pavement. Dad fainted while carrying a heavy box, and we revived him by making him drink a Coca-Cola. Mom kept complaining that she had rivers of sweat accumulating underneath her breasts and that her perm was being dissolved. The severe heat also caused our apart-ment building's sewer system to bubble up or something, which had Mom walking around with an *actual clothespin* on her nose so as to not inhale the stench: a true master of the-atrics. I personally didn't care that the whole place stunk like fecal matter, I had an actual home that wasn't a motel room. Plus, our apartment building had a community pool and a playground with a sandbox, where I'd eventually contract lice and go on to spread them to my entire family.

For the first few months we didn't have any furniture. We slept on mattresses on the ground, used an empty cardboard box as a dinner table, and mostly ate McDonald's meals that came in Styrofoam containers and chicken-flavored Top Ramen that also came in styrofoam containers (we may have been poor, but, as a family, we were single-handedly keeping Big Styrofoam alive).

I started school halfway through the year, just after I turned six. My parents enrolled me in Andasol Avenue Elementary. Some Argentines they'd met in the Valley advised Mom and Dad that this specific school had an excellent ESL program. (It really was wonderful to see how the community of Argentine expats supported one another, whether it was helping take care of each other's children; passing around clothing and furniture they no longer needed; giving the new, younger couples useful information, like what credit cards had the lowest APR; and warning each other about avoiding the bakery that was owned by a fellow Argentine because, allegedly, someone had bought a birthday cake from there and when they cut it open, a thousand maggots came crawling out of the frosting.)

The day I walked up to the entrance of my new school, I felt equal parts terror and excitement. Actually, it was mostly terror and very little excitement. The outside of the school had this mural painted on it depicting these really unfriendly-looking black horses that looked like they were about to charge right at me in a violent stampede. There was also a giant flagpole with an American flag waving at the top. "I live in the United States of America," I thought on my first day of class, as I stared up at that tall metal rod that looked like it went all the way up to the heavens. (I've always felt nostalgic for the entrance of this school. So much so that, in the present day, I decided to get stoned and drive back there to see what it looked like. More than thirty years had passed, and, to be quite honest, when I pulled up and rolled down the window, that flagpole looked short as hell and those scary black horses looked more like obese cows. They had words like "Friendship," "Sharing," and "Kindness" written across their bodies. I found this so funny that I started taking pictures of the murals from my car. I was so focused on taking photos that I didn't realize there was a woman approaching my vehicle. She looked pissed. That's when it dawned on me that I'd been sitting in my car like a fucking creep, taking photos of an elementary school full of young children. "Why are you taking pictures of the children, ma'am?" the angry mother yelled at me while writing my license plate number down. I was way too fucking high to explain that I attended the school as a kid and blah, blah, blah. Instead, I rolled my window up and peeled off like a psycho.)

My English as a second language class consisted of learning basic words such as "Dog, Happy, Friends, Potatoes, and Pain," and then putting all those words together by using what our teacher referred to as "glue words." Some of these glue words were "I, The, A, Have, Get, For, and Is." At first, I would mix and match random words without really caring what they meant, saying a lot of things like "The dog have happy get" or "I am a pain potato the." (Sometimes I feel like I still speak like this, even thirty years later.) There were immigrant children from all over the world in my class. Kids from China to Afghanistan. That classroom was the fucking tower of Babel.

I quickly became really good friends with a boy who spoke Spanish. His name was Francisquito, and he was from a city in Colombia, Medellín. He had fat cheekies that I would pinch, and sometimes bite, and he was my favorite (and only) friend, even though he put bananas in his spaghetti, which I thought was weird. There was another boy in my class from El Salvador named Esteban who spoke Spanish. He was a problem child. Me and Francisquito hated him because he never stood still and was always trying to get attention by doing things like putting needles under his skin or flipping his eyelids inside out, which made us sick. "My mom told me that Esteban has problems because he is adopted," Francisquito warned me on my first day of school. The poor boy thought he was Spiderman and was always climbing up furniture. Then, one day, he fell from the top of a really tall cabinet and broke both his arms. It was kind of funny at first. Francisquito and I laughed our asses off like the two garbage people that we were. Then, we realized the boy had bones popping out of places they shouldn't be popping out of and we started crying like pussies.

Sometimes Mom and Francisquito's mom would arrange playdates. They'd take us to the park and push us on the swings because neither of us had many toys in our homes to play with, being that we were newly arrived immigrants. And then, Francisquito's parents decided to go back to Colombia because they missed their family and felt too lonely in the United States. I never saw him again. I still think about Francisquito way more than I should. A few years ago, I even tried putting bananas in my spaghetti just like he did. Not bad at all. I've thought about looking for him online, but the only thing I know about him is that his name was Francisquito, and that really won't get me anywhere. All I have left of him is a picture of the two of us dangling from some monkey bars looking really smiley and happy.

I was so depressed by the loss of my friend that my ESL teacher agreed to let me take our class pet, Robby the Tadpole, home with me for a week. Robby the Tadpole lived in a giant Carlo Rossi bottle. "That frog is disgusting and it's going to give us serious diseases," Mom said when I walked into our apartment with it and placed it on the kitchen counter. But I loved waking up in the morning and watching that slimy little cornichon swim around in his wine jug. He was my new amphibian companion. One bummer of an afternoon, however, I came home from school to find that Robby wasn't in his bottle. I told Dad, and we desperately searched every corner of the apartment for him. We eventually realized Dad had stepped on it and murdered it when we found the thing completely flattened out on the bottom of his sneaker. Fuck. "First Francisquito leaves. Now Robby is dead," I cried as Dad wrapped what was left of it in a piece of tissue paper and flushed it down the toilet while saying a Jewish prayer that people say when a loved one passes.

And then, just a couple of months after I started ESL, I woke up one morning and I knew how to speak English almost perfectly. It was like magic. From one day to the next I was fluent. "My name is Tamara. I have six years olds and I came to America in an airplane," I said to my ESL teacher one day. I was missing my two front teeth and spoke in a thick Argentine accent.

"Very good, Tamara!" she answered. "Tell me more about yourself."

"Well," I continued, "I get so many friends in America! I get some big friends. I get some little friends. I get some, um, dead friends, and I get some beautiful friends." I had a few grammatical issues to work out, but who cared. I'm also assuming the dead friend was Robby the Tadpole. As for the big friends, little friends, and the beautiful friends . . . they didn't exist, but I'd repeat this line over and over again. I was manifesting. Nevertheless, that day, the teacher deemed me fluent, and I said goodbye to my classmates and was moved into a regular, non-ESL, first-grade class.

Soon enough, life in the States finally started to feel normal. Our apartment had furniture, my room was full of toys, we were going out to eat at gorgeous places like Sizzler. We even got to go to Universal Studios, where my parents paid for my sister and me to get our picture taken and super-imposed on the cover of a fake magazine titled something along the lines of "Perfect Dolls Magazine." Unfortunately, our Universal Studios visit was cut short after my sister tripped and fell while running around the Fievel the Mouse attraction and broke her perfect dollface, shattering her front teeth.

Finally I had adapted at school, where I actually *did* make all those beautiful friends I had manifested. And guess what? My parents made some beautiful friends of their own. Even though Dad worked what felt like twelve jobs (including his courier job, his job delivering newspapers, and another job where he went to people's houses and sharpened their knives), Mom and Dad's social life was thriving. They now had a huge community of about thirty Argentines who would do everything together.

Mom was loving life. (The only time I saw her get upset again was when one of her girlfriends named Ruth, who had bulgy eyes and looked like a goblin, came over, and the two of them got into a screaming fight. I guess Ruth had purposely not invited Mom to her birthday party at El Torito, which made Mom feel left out. I was in the living room, trying to drown out the screams by singing my favorite song of the moment, "It Must Have Been Love," by Roxette. I could feel the pain of the singer every time she belted "But it's over now," and tried as hard as I could to emulate that emotion with my own voice. Eventually Ruth came out of the room crying, snapping me out of my musical trance. "Look what your mother did!" she said to me, then showed me a tiny, bloody scratch on her cheek.)

Other than that little moment of rage, Mom was great. Every Saturday morning I'd accompany her to the nail salon where she'd get her acrylics done, and then we'd attend some sort of picnic or birthday party. I loved Mom and Dad's new friends. My favorite of all of them was an Argentine couple named Dina and Freddy Moldavsky. Dina and Freddy lived an hour away, in a place called Orange County, but they came to the Valley to visit us every weekend and they always brought their daughter, Bianca. Me and Bianca were best friends. We danced to Paula Abdul's "Opposites Attract," made our Barbies sit on each other's faces, and stuck out our tongues and made them touch each other.

As great as things were during this time of my life, the one thing that I lacked were my grandparents. I missed them so much, especially Pocho. Even though I'd eaten all the salami slices like he asked me to eat, he still hadn't come to visit. He'd broken his promise. We, in turn, weren't able to visit them in Argentina because we didn't have green cards, which meant that if we left the United States, we wouldn't be able to come back for a long time.

When I was halfway through first grade, I came home from school, and Mom told me she had some news to give me. I'd had a particularly shitty day because this boy in my class who was always making fun of my accent walked up to me at lunch and told me that he "wanted to eat my boobies with mayonnaise and salt." I don't even know where to begin with that. "I'll give you this news," Mom said, "but first let's go on a little walk." I started getting a bad feeling, like something had happened to one of my grandparents. There was a girl in my class whose grandfather had recently fallen off the roof of his house while putting up Christmas lights and had cracked his skull on the sidewalk and died. Mom held my hand as we exited our apartment. We walked no more than ten steps when she stopped at the door of the apartment that was directly next to ours. "What are we doing here?" I asked. The neighbor's door slowly opened, and, lo and behold, Pocho was standing right there in front of my very eyes. I didn't understand anything that was happening. "What are you doing here? Are you here on vacation?" I asked as he picked me up and spun me around in the air. I was crying from happiness. Rita and Sandra, my mom's older sister, were there too. I could tell by the looks on their faces that they weren't quite as thrilled to be there as Pocho was, but whatever.

"It's more than a vacation," Pocho answered. "We live here now. We're your new next-door neighbors."

Sexy Chicken

One month after my grandparents and aunt immigrated to the United States, my parents got into an abysmal argument that I will never forget. I'd most certainly rank it as one of their top ten fights. (Another one of these arguments that made it to the top ten, even top five, had occurred just a few years before, when Dad tried to install a three-hundred-pound jacuzzi tub in the backyard on his own. Mom warned him that it was too heavy and that he'd hurt himself, but he didn't listen and ended up dropping it on his big toe, leaving it dangling by a single tendon.) These arguments usually peaked in a crescendo of screaming then died down, leaving the entire household in a somber, quiet mood for the remainder of the day (and sometimes the day after).

This specific argument, however, happened because Dad was sour as fuck that Pocho had followed us to the United States and moved in DIRECTLY next door to us, and Mom had done nothing to stop him. "We left Buenos Aires to get some distance from our parents," he told Mom, "and now I can hear your Dad's voice through the wall every time I'm jerking off." Another thing that pissed Dad off was that the moment Pocho arrived in the United States, he began criticizing the fact that my dad worked what Pocho considered "shitty jobs," and started busting Dad's balls about how he should be owning his own business. At first, Dad pretended like Pocho's opinions didn't matter. He was happy delivering newspapers and sharpening knives. But it didn't take long for those comments to get to him. Dad started feeling the need to prove to Pocho that he *could*, in fact, open up his own small business, and started looking into getting loans. The only issue was that Mom and Dad couldn't figure out what kind of business to open. A children's clothing shop? A convenience store? A butcher shop? Not only did none of these things feel right, but whatever ideas Mom had, Dad hated, and whatever ideas Dad had, Mom instantly pooh-poohed. They'd been arguing about it all day, and the vibe was most definitely off. So Mom and Dad put me and my sister in the car and drove us to the one place where we'd always go when we needed to cool off: the mall.

It should be known that going to the mall has, and continues to be, my family's favorite thing to do, ever. It's where we go to calm down. Malls put us in zen mode. My parents have been obsessed with malls for as long as I can remember, and so have I. Maybe it's because my parents are children of merchants. They were raised inside of stores, and they feel safe in places where people go to spend their hard-earned cash. For their honeymoon, my parents went to Miami and spent the majority of their trip locked inside the Aventura Mall looking for deals instead of relaxing on the beach. They spent so much time inside the mall, with its intense air-conditioning system blasting on them, that my dad got pneumonia.

When I was a baby, the surest way to get me to calm down whenever I had a fit of crying was to take me to Unicenter, Buenos Aires's biggest mall. It was located thirty minutes outside the city, but they'd put me in my stroller, push me around the mall, and within seconds I'd stop crying and fall asleep. The mall was my pacifier. Even today, if I'm ever in a bad place mentally, you better believe I'm not going to a yoga class: I'm going to walk around the Glendale Galleria to clear my head.

The majority of the people I know fucking hate going to the mall, and that makes me sad. They see it as a chore, a punishment. When they *do* visit a mall, they try to get in and out as quickly as possible, treating the whole experience as an errand. They'll walk directly to J.Crew, where they purchase the single white button-up they need for the wedding they're attending later that evening, then quickly head back to their cars, ignoring all the beauty they pass along the way. They're like horses with blinders on.

But my family and I come alive when we enter those massive chunks of cement. The moment that fresh mall oxygen enters our system and pumps through our bloodstream, we become intoxicated. Inside malls, we walk with a purpose. Our postures improve. We become Kate Mosses. Under the bright neon lights of a mall, we shine just like the vampires from *Twilight* when they step out into daylight. Inside malls we are so beautiful. You would agree with me if you saw my mother gliding toward Macy's when she knows a 70-percent-off sale awaits her. I saw this happen not long ago. Her feet were moving so quickly over the freshly buffed white tile, it looked like she was floating.

But back to that day in 1990. As we strolled around the newly renovated Fallbrook mall in West Hills, my parents finally came to an agreement and decided that they should start a business inside it. This decision was made in the food court and came to them thanks to the fact that I threw a horrible temper tantrum. What happened was that mom asked me what food court stand I wanted to eat from. "You want pizza? Chinese food? A salad from the Build Your Own Salad stand?"

"I don't want any of those options," I yelled, throwing a fit. "I want El Pollo Loco!"

The thing is, I had recently tasted the perfection that was El Pollo Loco for the first time, and it immediately became my favorite place to eat in the whole wide world. I loved everything about El Pollo Loco. I loved the way the air in there smelled: thick and salty. I loved the way you could watch those beautiful golden chickens spin around as they cooked. I loved that they gave you your very own pack of flour or corn tortillas, and that you could take some rice, beans, and salsa and build yourself your very own mini-taquito. All this to say that, on this specific day, we were faced with a problem: There was no El Pollo Loco at the Fallbrook mall food court.

I was seven years old when I threw this temper tantrum, and it wasn't the first I'd thrown. A few years earlier, when we were still in Argentina, I threw a pretty concerning tantrum while my mom was helping me get ready because my uncle Raul was about to take me and my cousin to see a live taping of the children's hit television show *El Show de Carlitos Balá*. Carlitos Balá was my idol: an Argentine man in his sixties who had a severe bowl cut and wore black leather overalls so tight that you could kind of see the outline of his balls and penis. Carlitos sang psychedelic songs inspired by the Beatles'

Sergeant Pepper era, except they were about how to kick your pacifier habit, or how to treat your bus driver with respect. He was known for his catchphrase, "What does salt taste like?" A phrase he would kick off his shows with by asking it before an audience made up entirely of children, who in unison would answer, "It tastes salty!!!" (I decided to take a one-minute break from writing this to google Carlitos Balá, and the "one minute" turned into me going down an hourlong rabbit hole that included finding out Carlitos recently died of natural causes at the age of ninety-seven and going on to purchase every biography that was ever written about him.)

Anyways, as my uncle Raul was about to pick me up, I freaked the fuck out because I had set my mind on wanting to wear a red T-shirt with a pocket on it to the live taping of this show. That's because earlier that day, while I was watching Alf on TV, I noticed that Lynn Tanner (Alf's human sister) was wearing a red T-shirt with a pocket on it, and she looked so pretty and cool that I wanted to look just like her. My thought process was that the only way I was going to get noticed by Carlitos Balá and be brought up on the stage to sing a song with him was if I wore a red T-shirt with a pocket on it. (Looking back, it seems to me that both Carlitos Balá and the red T-shirt didn't matter, per se. They were simply a means to an end that would help me achieve my true and ultimate goal: Getting on a goddamn stage and being seen.)

The problem was that I didn't own a red T-shirt with a pocket on it. As my mom helped me get dressed, she offered me alternatives that were hanging up in my closet. A red skirt with ruffles? A red sweater with Strawberry Shortcake on it? A green T-shirt with a pocket on it? Hell no, none of those options were good enough to get me on that stage with my dear Carlitos. I began scratching and kicking, and even attempted to bite the head off a Care Bear stuffed animal that was lying around. I wanted a red T-shirt with a pocket on it, and I wanted it NOW!

I never made it to the Carlitos Balá show. It was my first taste of failing at being a star. The temper tantrum I threw that morning was so incredibly upsetting to my parents that they ended up throwing me in a cold shower until I calmed down, and then putting me in behavioral therapy for a couple of months.

Now, let us return to the Fallbrook mall. As I screamed and kicked because I wanted El Pollo Loco at the Fallbrook mall food court, my parents looked at each other and said, "She's onto something here. There really isn't an El Pollo Loco at the Fallbrook mall food court. Maybe we should open our version of it." They had finally agreed on something!

While I banged against the food court table, my parents riffed on what their version of El Pollo Loco could be. El Pollo Cool? El Pollo Gordo? El Pollo Argentino? El Pollo Chicken? Nothing felt right. They wanted something spectacular, something that would draw crowds. A new kind of *Pollo* that the world had never seen. And that's when my parents were interrupted by a woman's high-pitched voice. "You usin' this extra chair?" she said. When they looked up, they saw a voluptuous woman who oozed sexuality out of every pore in her body. She had teased blonde hair and a low-cut, black leather dress that showed off her perfect, fake tits.

"Go ahead," my parents answered her. "Take the chair." They then looked at each other and knew what our version of El Pollo Loco would be. That's how "Sexy Chicken" was born.

The Feral Child of the Mall

In the days leading up to Sexy Chicken's grand opening, Mom and Dad hired a friend of theirs (who used to be a pretty well-known fashion designer in Argentina, but now worked at a movie theater in the Valley, serving popcorn and sodas) to design a sign and logo for our new store. The sign read SEXY CHICKEN in big, red, block letters. Next to the name stood a seductive, cartoon rotisserie chicken smoking a cigarette. The chicken, who was a female of course, had big blonde hair, wore a tight black leather dress, and had an obscenely large pair of round ones. As for the food of it all, Mom and Dad poached a cook from El Pollo Loco who agreed to come work for us and bring all of the restaurant's recipes with him. We were set.

To my father's dismay, three months after Sexy Chicken's grand opening, Pocho went ahead and opened up his own store in the Fallbrook mall, just a couple of steps away from

Dad's food court stand. Pocho named his store "Fancy Stationery," and it sold children's toys and all things Sanrio.

My dad may have wanted to slit his wrists, but I was in
heaven. That summer vacation I spent all day at the mall. I'd
hit up Sexy Chicken and help the cook season the raw chickens in the kitchen during the lunch rush. He'd then make me
a burrito, and I'd walk over to my grandparents' store like I
owned the place. Rita and Sandra worked the registers at
Fancy Stationery and were always pretty busy ringing up customers. Meanwhile, I helped Pocho merchandise the store and
restock items that had sold out. While we filled up the shelves
with goodies, I taught Grandpa words in English. In return,
he taught me words in Yiddish, which he said was "the beautiful language of our ancestors." He introduced me to rich
Yiddish words like *drek*, which means "shit," *petzl*, which
means "a man's penis," *schmuck*, which means "a man's penis,"
schlepper, which means "someone who's a bum and is badly
dressed," and *putz*, which means "someone who is stupid," but
also means "a man's penis." Lots of words for penis in Yiddish.

Things seemed to be going well for a while, and there was
even talk of us moving out of our apartment and buying our
own house. And then, not even a year after the openings of
Sexy Chicken and Fancy Stationery, my parents and grandparents began complaining that their stores weren't making
any money. The words *Gulf War* were frequently thrown
around at home. The Gulf War is making the oil prices impossible. The Gulf War is causing people to be careful with their
money, and now they're scared to come spend it at the mall.
The Gulf War is the reason we're not selling any chicken.

I was seven at the time, and I thought the war had been
caused by a condiment. I'll explain. In Argentina we had our

own version of Thousand Island, which we referred to as "Salsa Golf," which is basically just mayonnaise mixed with ketchup. The word *Gulf* sounded like *Golf*, so I was certain that some country far, far away was trying to steal all the other countries' Salsa Golf, and that was the reason we were fighting the war. Children's brains are so beautiful.

From one day to the next, however, the Fallbrook mall became a ghost town. A deserted depression of a building. On those final days of summer before beginning second grade, I would visit Sexy Chicken and watch my parents stand around, waiting for customers who never arrived. Business owners didn't even bother being inside their businesses anymore. Dad and the owners of the Chinese food stand and the Build Your Own Salad stand would congregate outside their restaurants and argue over which of them had made the fewest sales that day. It was like a contest over who took the least amount of money home. "Sexy Chicken made thirty-two dollars yesterday," Dad would tell his fellow business owners.

"That's a goddamn fortune, Marcos," the Build Your Own Salad guy would answer. "All I sold yesterday was a medium Diet Coke." Meanwhile, I sat at the food court tables eating as many mini-taquitos as my stomach could handle, thinking I was helping my parents by consuming the chicken so it wouldn't go bad.

When I wasn't at the food court, I'd explore the dying mall alone. I would greet the various shop owners, who all knew me by name. The pretty girls from Orange Julius, who would give me as many free juicies as I wanted and even let me go behind the counter and pour my own drinks if the manager wasn't around. The teenage boy with cystic acne who worked at the video game store where I bought my first Nintendo would wave at me as I passed and say, "See ya tomorrow, Tamara." Even the old woman who was mean to everyone and never smiled would invite me to come into her clothing boutique, Diva's Fashions, and let me rub the cashmere pashminas and silk scarves all over my face. I was the feral child of the Fallbrook mall.

Finally, I'd arrive at my grandparents' store. Since there were no shoppers, I pretended to be one, thinking I was helping them by keeping them occupied. I'd grab a basket, fill it with merchandise, and present it to Rita, who was always smoking cigarettes behind the cash register, reading the same Argentine gossip magazine she'd been reading since she arrived more than one year earlier. "I would like to purchase these items," I'd say to her, even though I had no way of paying for them.

"Just take them," she replied, taking a drag of her cigarette. "We're never gonna sell any of this shit anyways."

On one occasion, a woman who was standing near JCPenney holding a clipboard and wearing a cool vest with a rainbow-colored apple on it asked me if I wanted to be part of a focus group for the new Apple computer. When she inquired if my mom was around and would be okay with me participating in this trial, I told her it wouldn't be a problem because my parents owned the mall. She took me and a few other people into an empty store that had nothing but desks and computers in it, and I got to press the buttons on a computer for the first time in my life. She then asked me a bunch of questions about my experience with this Apple computer and gave me a twenty-dollar gift certificate that could be used at any store in the mall.

That afternoon, I skipped back to the food court and handed Dad the gift certificate. When he asked me how I got it, I told him I found it on the ground. It was probably his biggest profit that day.

Not long after, it became clear to my parents that maintaining Sexy Chicken was unsustainable, and Dad started picking up night-time newspaper delivery shifts again. Mom and Dad began discussing giving up the business. They could either close it and lose all the money they'd invested or try to find someone to sell it to and find new jobs. So when a friend of my parents mentioned that she knew a really wealthy man named Alex who was interested in taking over an already existing food stand, they hoped that this was their chance.

When my parents first spoke to Alex, he told them he didn't want anything that would be too hard to run. He wanted a stand his wife could operate because she was bored at home after all their children had gone to college. He didn't care about making tons of money, but more so wanted to give his wife something to do. Before purchasing the business, Alex wanted to come by and scope out the food stand to see how busy it got.

My parents thought that if this man came by and saw how poorly the food stand performed, he'd never take it over. So on the day Alex was coming to check out the business, they devised a plan to get every single person they knew to pay a visit to Sexy Chicken and pretend to be a customer.

That day, as our potential buyer looked on from a nearby table, he witnessed a steady flow of dozens of customers patiently waiting in line to place an order at their favorite food court stand, Sexy Chicken. The line, of course, consisted of dedicated hired actors including Pocho, Rita, a few neighbors from our apartment complex, a large crowd of Mom and Dad's Argentine friends, including the Moldavskys and my aunt Sandra, who brought her new boyfriend along with her, a really handsome Mexican guy named Mateo, whom she'd met while salsa dancing one weekend. Alex looked totally impressed by how well the business did. We had accomplished our mission. We had fooled him.

That evening, me and my family sat at the dinner table waiting for Alex's call while *Back to the Future* played on TV. My parents were already celebrating the sale of the business when Alex called to inform us that he was backing out. "Why would you ever want to get rid of that gold mine, Marcos?" He told Dad over the phone, "I'm a fool for not buying it, but Sexy Chicken is just too busy and demanding of a business. I wanted something a little slower paced. My wife is too lazy, she won't be able to handle that many customers on her own."

Dad hung up and passed on the bad news to Mom, right as Marty McFly remembered how to play "Earth Angel" on the guitar during his parents' "Enchantment Under the Sea" school dance. While Marty's mother and father kissed passionately on the dance floor, my mother fell to her knees and began banging her fist on our beige-carpeted floors, screaming, "We don't deserve this much bad luck. What are we, cockroaches?" My father, realizing that she was having some sort of breakdown, kneeled behind her and held her. I stared at the television, thinking "I wish I had a perfect all-American life like Marty McFly" while my mom rocked back and forth on her knees repeating the phrase "What are we, cockroaches?"

A few days later, as I was starting second grade, I took it upon myself to fix the Sexy Chicken problem. I thought, if only we got more sales—and I'm talking real sales, not friends and family pretending to be customers—then maybe the food stand wouldn't close down. So when I came home from school, I told Mom I was going over to Pocho and Rita's apartment. Instead, I took my bike to the section of the apartment building that was farther away. I parked my bike and walked up to a random apartment. I knocked on the door, and a nice old lady opened. "Can I help you, sweetheart?" she asked.

"Good afternoon," I answered in my sassiest, most charming voice, while placing my hands on my hip. "I'm here to tell you to visit Sexy Chicken at the Fallbrook mall food court. It's the tastiest AND sexiest chicken in town!"

"Uh, okay darling, I will," replied the old lady, quickly shutting her door in my face. Proud that I had recruited one customer, I went on to the next apartment.

"I'm here to tell you to visit Sexy Chicken at the Fallbrook mall food court. It's the tastiest AND sexiest chicken in town!" Over and over, I advertised our business, door to door, to confused adults, teenagers, and children.

After about five or six apartments, I decided to try my luck on one of the upstairs units. I knocked on the door, but could hear that there was music blasting inside, so I knocked harder. Just when I was about to walk away, a man opened the door. He was wearing basketball shorts and a shirt that had the sleeves cut off. I'm guessing he was in his thirties. "Can I help you?" he asked, talking over the loud music that was playing inside.

"Visit Sexy Chicken at the Fallbrook mall food court. It's the tastiest AND sexiest chicken in town!" I said, kind of scared, and losing a little bit of the sass and enthusiasm that I had in the previous apartments.

"What's your name?" the man said.

"Tamara . . ." I answered.

"Do you wanna come inside, Tamara?" he asked. "I'm about to feed my pet snake." Saying no just didn't feel like an option, so I hesitantly walked into the man's home.

The apartment had the exact same layout as the one I lived in, except all the light bulbs were emitting a red light, and it smelled like a dirty pet store. The man walked me over to a big, empty fish tank where a four-foot snake was curled up. "He's starving," the man said as he pulled out a frozen mouse from his freezer and defrosted it in the microwave for a couple of minutes. It made the already stanky apartment take on an even worse smell of burnt fur. The man then returned to the snake and dropped the limp, thawed-out mouse into the tank. The snake didn't look interested at first. But then it slowly made its way over to the mouse and devoured it in a single bite. As I watched the lump make its way down the snake's body, all I could think about was Cinderella's best friends Jaq and Gus, the sweet mice that helped her make her gown for the ball, and I wanted to get the hell out of that apartment.

Next, the man invited me to his living room, where I sat on his black leather couch, which had tears all over it that had been taped with silver duct tape. He turned on the TV, and we watched music videos together. We may have sat there for five minutes or an hour. I don't recall exactly how long, but I was a seven-year-old child hanging out with a thirty-something man, and it was starting to get dark outside. "I have to go home, my mom is going to get worried," I told him.

"Promise me you'll come visit me again." I promised I would. The man then walked me to his door. He let me out, and I got on my bike and rode home so fast I flew off the bicycle and skinned my knees.

Despite my best efforts, there was no point in me trying to save Sexy Chicken. That's because, while I was out on my advertising rampage, my family's fate had already been decided for us. Earlier that day, Dad had received a call from Nilda letting him know that his father had been feeling strange for the past few months, and they'd just returned from the doctor where he'd been diagnosed with colon cancer. During that phone call, Nilda implied to Dad that Benjamín's cancer had been caused by the fact that we left Argentina and abandoned them. "Come back to your family where you belong and make right by your father," she demanded on the phone. To sweeten the deal, she told my dad that he could take over my grandfather's textile-manufacturing business. Without asking Mom what she thought of this, he agreed. A month later, we were on our way back to Buenos Aires.

PART III

Back to Argentina

YIDDISHLAND

The week before we moved back to Argentina, Dad put all our belongings into a shipping container that was set to depart from the Port of San Pedro, in Los Angeles, and arrive at the Port of Buenos Aires a couple of weeks later. He was assured that it would take no more than two weeks. Maybe three. Absolutely not a day longer than four weeks. Dad figured that it'd be more cost-efficient to have the furniture from our place in Northridge sent to our new apartment in Buenos Aires, rather than having to buy brand-new stuff. Mind you, we didn't have an apartment in Buenos Aires yet. But he'd rent one right away. He wanted us to have a more seamless move this time around. As opposed to three years earlier, when we arrived in Los Angeles with nothing. Sure, his attempt at establishing a life in the United States may have turned out to be a failure, but at least we'd be returning to Argentina with furniture. We wouldn't have to start from zero this time.

No more sleeping on mattresses on the ground. No more cardboard boxes for tables.

And so, the entire contents of our apartment set sail across the Pacific Ocean. Our black Jacquard sofa set with peach accent pillows. The glass dining table with wicker chairs that we bought for 50 percent off at Kmart. The collection of toys my sister and I had acquired. Even the framed poster, which hung above my bed, of my sweetheart Kevin Costner, posing sensually with his hairy chest on display.

Dad's plan was for us to live at Nilda and Benjamín's two-bedroom apartment for a couple of weeks, and for the four of us to sleep in the two twin beds from his childhood bedroom. He wouldn't have to worry about work because he was promised a job managing his father's thriving textile business where he was guaranteed, according to Nilda, to be "picking up thousand-dollar bills with shovels." He'd then rent an apartment for us, and we'd move in just as our container arrived. Easy.

Mom wasn't as confident. She didn't want to return in the first place. She loved living in the United States. She loved the clean roads of Los Angeles, the palm trees, the way you could trust your mail not to be stolen from your mailbox, and the clearance section at the JCPenney Outlet, where items were so heavily discounted, she claimed that they were "basically free." Most of all, though, she loved being far away from Nilda. The moment she set foot in her mother-in-law's apartment, and she smelled the rancid stench of mothballs emanating from the closets, saw the mold on the bathroom ceilings and the twin beds where we'd be sleeping, which were illuminated by a single flickering light bulb, she was hit with a wave of gloom and misery. Mom then heard Nilda's high-pitched voice babying my father, asking if he wanted her to "draw him a bath," and fell into a state of depression so severe that she contemplated the idea of swallowing an entire bag of mothballs, and for two days she refused to eat, speak, or move from her tiny bed. Mom, whose usual coping mechanism was rage, had become completely catatonic, and that was somehow scarier for Dad. That's why, forty-eight hours after our arrival, he realized that staying at Nilda's apartment was not going to be feasible and made the executive decision to temporarily move us into Nilda's "summer home." A home located outside Buenos Aires, in a country club by the name of "Yiddishland."

I know the words *country club* make it sound like Yiddishland was some sort of upper-crust summer destination with gorgeous homes that sat alongside a golf course, but that's not what it was. Yiddishland was a retirement community for Jews made up of little apartments, one of which Nilda inherited from a brother who had passed. It was a summer home where one went to die.

Yiddishland was forty-five minutes outside Buenos Aires. It was the middle of nowhere, in what reminded me of the woods where Hansel and Gretel get lost and come across the cottage of a cannibal witch. There were no supermarkets, bars, or restaurants nearby. You would simply drive through an unnamed dirt road until you reached a gate with guardrails that eerily resembled the entrance to Auschwitz, except the word *YIDDISHLAND* was written across in block letters. On arrival, a guard who was holding a rifle for some reason would check your ID and grant you access to the club. In addition to the residences, it had amenities like a cafeteria that served year-round soup for breakfast, lunch, and dinner, a small pool dirty with moss that always had a film of slime on it, and a community room where they hosted Rummikub and bridge tournaments, and the occasional movie night.

Mom, Dad, my sister, and I ended up living in Yiddishland for almost two months. We had no phone or TV, and we didn't have a car, which meant we could never leave and were almost completely disconnected from the outside world. Since we couldn't go to the supermarket to buy groceries, we were forced to eat all our meals at the cafeteria. We couldn't visit friends, and we most definitely couldn't go to the mall. Mom continued to resent Dad; she would avert her eyes whenever she spoke to him. But her depression was beginning to improve. Eventually, the four of us became closer than we'd ever been. We were all we had. We'd go to water aerobics classes in the nasty pool with all the senior citizens, we'd go on walks, and we'd attend movie nights in the social room where we watched uplifting films like *Yentl* and *Sophie's Choice*.

The level of boredom I experienced during my stay at Yiddishland was so acute that I found myself talking to squirrels. Since there were no kids my age to play with, I saw myself forced to expand my horizons when it came to friendships. This led me to make one of the best friends I've ever had. Her name was Rosita Rabinovich, but everyone called her "Bubaleh." Bubaleh was in her seventies, and she lived two doors down from us at Yiddishland. The first thing that drew me to Bubaleh was her boisterous laugh. The joy that woman spread with her contagious cackling was something I wanted to partake in. For days, I lurked, hiding behind trees, spying on Bubaleh as she and other old ladies played Rummikub on a plastic table outside her apartment, laughing maniacally at who knows what. I thought she couldn't see me, but one day she called me over.

"Hey you, girlie. Stop hanging around like a mosquito and come learn how to play Rumi."

"Yes!" I answered, desperately. I was in with the most popular girl in the community.

My new friend took a liking to me instantly. She dedicated countless hours to helping me master this game, which was the preferred activity for Jewish women over sixty. A game that was created by a Romanian Jew during the 1950s, outlawed by the communists, and which we played with elegant tiles made out of elephant tusks. I got so good at Rummikub that Bubaleh enrolled me in one of the Yiddishland tournaments. Not only did I win third place after kicking Bubaleh's ass, but I was also given a special trophy for being the youngest contestant in the club's history.

Bubaleh wasn't only *my* friend. My parents fell in love with her too, and she became a part of the family. My dad started saying that he had "three daughters: Tamara who is nine, the little one who is five, and Bubaleh who is seventy-two." Bubaleh ate every meal with us in the cafeteria. She would invite us over to her apartment to watch VHS tapes of the *Looney Tunes*. She fucking LOVED *Looney Tunes* and would legitimately cry of laughter every time Wile E. Coyote got run over by a tractor or got smashed by a swinging ball. We, in turn, would invite Bubaleh over for sleepovers where she slept uncomfortably on our couch, even though her own bedroom was two doors down. We were like a little cult.

Despite her joy, Bubaleh's story was a sad one. She had been sent to Yiddishland by her only son, who refused to visit her or answer her calls after her husband died of a heart attack.

She was a lonely, retired seamstress of Polish descent who kept dozens of framed pictures of all her dead relatives on a credenza, which she referred to as her "cemetery." She had rosy pink cheeks, was heavyset, wore flip-flops that smacked loudly against the ground whenever she took a step, and had the most giant tits I've ever seen in my life. Her breasts were so large she had to make her own bras by sewing extra fabric onto existing bras. Bubaleh's breasts brought me an indescribable motherly comfort. I loved Bubaleh's breasts so much that my favorite thing to do was stick my face between them and motorboat them. "It's tittie timeeeee!" I'd yell, then face-plant into her bosom and breathe in the soothing smell of baby powder. I'd often do this in front of my parents, and everyone would laugh. One day, I thought I'd take my joke a step further: I buried my face into Bubaleh and bit into one of her breasts. The bite was so deep I left little toothmarks above her areola. Bubaleh screamed from the pain, and my parents froze, and then yelled for me to "go to my room."

During my childhood, I got scolded a lot for this kind of thing. Not biting boobs, but trying to be funny by pushing boundaries. When I was five, I thought it would be hilarious to grab a knife from the kitchen, wave it in front of my little cousin's face, and threaten to kill him. No one found this amusing. In fact, they were so horrified that after sending me to my room for the remainder of the evening, they had me see yet another child psychologist who diagnosed me with developmental issues. Another time I thought I was being funny was when my mom took me to my pediatrician because I had a rash in my vagina. When the doctor asked me to pull down my pants because he was going to "examine my flower," I looked at him with a smug expression and said, "I don't have a flower, I have a pussy." My mom wanted to die of embarrassment, and when we came home from the doctor's office, she sent me to my room again. On all these occasions I loved being sent to my room. I felt cool and defiant. But after the incident with Bubaleh, I felt different: an empty sadness. Something I'd describe as a combination of self-pity and self-hatred. Not so much because I had just tried to bite a chunk of tit from a senior citizen, but because my parents and I shared a room at Yiddishland, which meant I didn't have a room of my own I could go to.

Our first few weekends at Yiddishland were the busiest. People came to see us by the dozens: uncles, aunts, friends of my parents who would bring their kids for me to play with. Me and my parents were a novelty: shiny new things that had just arrived from the United States. People were desperate to hear our stories. They were curious to know what it was like to earn dollars for a living, and wanted to hear me and my sister say things in English for them. There was one specific aunt of mine who drove me crazy with questions about the U.S. She had bleached blonde hair, and her nipple was always popping out of her shirt for some reason. She was always cornering me to ask how much things cost in the United States. "How many dollars does a hand towel cost in America?" or "How much does a retiree earn per month?" she'd ask. How the fuck was I supposed to know? I was seven.

Eventually, Nilda and Benjamín came to Yiddishland with extraordinary news. There was an apartment for rent that was only five blocks away from theirs and belonged to one of Nilda's friends, which meant we'd be getting a discount. It was available to move in as soon as possible, and, what's more, Nilda told us that she'd gotten a call from the shipping company informing her that the container with our furniture had finally arrived. Things were looking up! We'd finally be able to get out of our senior living limbo and start our life in Buenos Aires, in our own apartment, with our own furniture. Still, the mood was somber the next day when we repacked our suitcases, which hadn't even been fully unpacked. We had to say a devastating goodbye to our sweet Bubaleh, and then we headed back to Buenos Aires.

The first thing Dad did was make arrangements with the shipping company. Meanwhile, my sister, Mom, and I explored our new apartment. It was a dream, with two huge bedrooms, a playroom where we'd be able to put all our toys, a balcony, AND a patio, which was unfortunately being used as a trash can by all the neighbors who lived on the floors above us. Instead of disposing of their garbage in their own trash cans, our neighbors preferred opening their windows and dumping it out onto our balcony. We found all kinds of things on that balcony, like used tampons, maxi pads, cans, and spit wads. One time someone from one of the top floors let out a biblical scream, then chucked an entire roast chicken from their window, which flew through the air and smashed down on our patio. "People have no respect in this country," Mom cried, longing for the cleanliness and order of California. She then collected all the trash from our patio and passive-aggressively scattered it in the building's lobby, leaving behind a sign that read: "Dispose properly of your garbage, you sick animal sons of bitches." The trash dumping only got worse after that. But I didn't give a shit about the trash. I had a patio to play with and a playroom to fill with toys.

My joy was deflated, however, when Dad came home from the port. Even though the shipping container had, in fact, arrived, the port authorities wouldn't be able to hand over our furniture. Turns out we'd shared a container with a man who was exporting fake Christmas trees. When the container arrived, the man didn't have enough money to pay his shipping costs. So the shipping company told us they couldn't open our container until the man paid his part, and suggested Dad check back in about six months. We'd been screwed. Nilda drove Dad straight from the port to a furniture store where she purchased two twin mattresses for me and my sister and a full-size mattress for my parents. It wasn't until the next year that the Christmas tree man decided to pay what he owed, which meant that we once again lived without furniture for nine months.

The day our things arrived, my parents picked me up from school early because they had a surprise for me. When I opened the front door, it was all there! Our black sofa with peach accent pillows, the table we bought at Kmart, my sexy Kevin Costner poster, and all of my toys were perfectly set up in our playroom. I could tell that my parents were excited to see my reaction, to see me freak out over being reunited with my things and be able to provide some sense of stability for me. I did indeed freak out, but from a void-like, horrible sadness. As I walked from room to room, taking in my old-new belongings, I began to sob uncontrollably because I was witnessing the ghost of our life in the United States.

Soon after our furniture arrived, my parents threw a party at home to celebrate my eighth birthday. It was one of those rare days in which I felt cheerful. Not just because it was my birthday, but because Pocho and Rita had recently returned to Buenos Aires, once again following in our footsteps, which meant that I'd get to celebrate with all four of my grandparents. And then, just moments after I blew out the candles, my aunt whose nipple was always popping out of her shirt ran into the living room screaming because she noticed "some water" on the floor seeping in from the kitchen. And by some water, she meant a fuck-ton of water. Water that was cascading into the living room and flowing down the hallway that led to our bedrooms. Suddenly all the women at my birthday party were screaming as the men scrambled to figure out where this water was coming from. Until, finally, Dad realized that a pipe in our kitchen had burst.

The plumbers didn't arrive until the next day. By then, the apartment was completely flooded. It had gotten so bad that the floors were covered in three inches of water. We were living in a fucking pond. The plumbers told us the furniture was most likely salvageable, but we'd have to leave the apartment while they worked on draining it and replacing the carpets. Once more we were without a home. And so, Mom, Dad, my sister, and I threw a few articles of clothing into a weekend bag and had Nilda drive us back to Yiddishland for a couple of days. But this time, when we returned to the city, we brought Bubaleh back to live with us.

Like a Prayer

The first school my parents enrolled me in when we returned to Argentina was the Escuela Talmud Torá Harishono Dr. Herzl. In case it's not obvious, it was a Jewish school. I started the year halfway through second grade. It was the middle of a freezing winter, and our apartment didn't have a heater. Dad would wake me up at six thirty A.M., carry me out of bed and into the kitchen, where he'd turn on all the burners on the stove, and sit next to me, rubbing my arms and legs until I defrosted. We didn't have a car yet, so Dad would walk me to school in the rain, on streets made out of cracked cobblestones, cars splashing as they passed. I realize that this might sound picturesque. It wasn't. It sucked big eggs. Most days I arrived at school with my teeth chattering from the cold. I even developed a foul fungal infection on my toes from walking around with wet socks that made my feet smell sour, like vinegary cottage cheese.

In the mornings we studied the usual stuff, math, science, Argentine history. But the entire afternoon was dedicated to learning Hebrew and reading the Torah. I didn't know a single word in Hebrew, which meant that, for half the day, I had absolutely no idea what the fuck anyone around me was saying. I was completely lost. And that's when I learned the wonderful art of dissociation. While the rest of the kids sang songs in Hebrew and wrote letters in an alphabet I had never seen, I went into trances where I traveled back to the United States: I walked around the Fallbrook mall; I went to Universal Studios and rode the King Kong ride; I went to Chuck E. Cheese, where I played Skee-Ball and had enough tickets to buy myself a Super Mario bean bag chair. The level of detail that went into my dissociations was masterful. I was an artiste. And every time I went on these mental voyages, I would repeat a weird mantra in my head. I have no idea where it came from, but it was a sort of made-up language that went something like this: *Torokoooo, Sureteeee, Bondidichiiii Shokamamaaaa.* Over and over I repeated these words, while I traveled to far-off lands. *Torokoooo, Sureteeee, Bondidichiiii Shokamamaaaa.*

During my time at Dr. Herzl, I never complained. I never told my parents that I didn't have friends because the kids were all pale and depressed me, or that one bitchy girl in class pricked me with a safety pin and I just stood there staring at her without flinching. I was so numb that my parents once took me to get my haircut, and when the hairdresser washed my hair in scalding hot water that burned my scalp, I didn't tell him to make the water colder or say anything at all, preferring to let the pain pass through me like I wasn't there. It had been less than two years before that I'd had to learn

English and make friends in a brand-new school, and what was my reward for that? Getting hoisted out by a crane, uprooted, and moved to a new location. So what was the point of trying again? It was easiest to not complain and, mentally, go elsewhere.

I could have stayed on this path forever, with my eyes glazed over, content to be nonexistent. But about six months into the year my parents started to notice that something was up. It happened after they came to see me perform in a school play. I can't remember what the play was about because it was in Hebrew. But I played a flower, along with two other girls in my grade. Dad spent hours creating a gorgeous headpiece for me to wear that had huge petals made out of glittery construction paper. During this performance, me and the two girls were supposed to come out onstage and sing a song called "Dayenu," which was really fast and had a ton of words in it. The song was about the Jews experiencing slavery and suffering, so I have no idea why we were dressed like flowers, but when I came out onstage, I realized that I didn't know a single word to this song. Not even one. So while the girls sang and gracefully waved their arms in the air, I stood there dissociating with my mouth half open, staring straight at my family members, who were sitting in the audience. The part of me who once dreamed of dancing and singing for an audience had disappeared. Instead of being on that stage, I was taking a mental trip, traveling down the Pacific Coast Highway in a limousine that had a built-in jacuzzi in the back.

After the performance, we took a taxi back to our apartment, and my parents were completely silent the entire ride. When we got home, Dad asked me why I didn't sing along with the other girls during the show. He looked concerned, but also like he pitied me. "I'm shy," I said. He didn't buy it. "I mean, I forgot the words," I added. Another obvious lie.

"Well, why didn't you do any of the choreography, either? The other girls were dancing, waving their arms in the air, and you were just standing there. You scared us." I shrugged, unable to come up with an excuse. "What have you been doing in school this whole time, Tamara? Have you even learned any Hebrew?"

"Of course I have. I love the Torah and God," I answered.

"Then say something. Say anything in Hebrew," Dad demanded. I think my brain had completely rotted after not using it for six months. The only thing I could think of was to go into my made-up language, hoping that he would buy that this was Hebrew.

"Uhhh . . . *Torokoooo, Sureteeee, Bondidichiiii Shokamamaaaa.*"

My parents took me out of Dr. Herzl the next week and enrolled me in a more modern school called Lange Ley that specialized in English. I got off to a rocky start there, too, unfortunately. On my first day, I tripped while trying to climb over one of those chair-desk combos, and the metal bar that connected the two hit me right in the vagina. It was one of the worst pains I've ever experienced. Because it was my first day, I was scared and embarrassed to tell the teacher that I had injured myself. Instead, I asked for permission to go to the bathroom to see what was happening down there. In the stall, I pulled my pants down, terrified at what I'd find. And, of course, I was bleeding. A lot. The blood was reddish brown, and it had seeped through my pants, leaving a stain on my butt that looked like I had shit myself. I made it through the rest of the day holding back tears and pretending my vagina wasn't on fire, but when Mom picked me up, I broke down crying and told her about my accident. She took me straight to a doctor, who examined me and said that I had most likely broken my hymen.

Despite this vaginal setback, I was happy to have been moved to a school where half the day was in Spanish and the other half was dedicated to English. Sure, I already spoke perfect English, but it didn't matter; I desperately needed to be around something familiar, something that reminded me of my life in the U.S. My English teacher's name was Miss Lolita. She was an old woman with dyed red hair and extremely grown-out roots. She smelled like tangerines, and all the kids treated her like shit. Miss Lolita spoke English with a thick Argentine accent and had constant grammatical errors, which I had to stop myself from correcting, because I knew I'd come off as an asshole in front of the other kids. At Dr. Herzl I didn't understand anything; now I understood too much.

Even though I liked this school better, I was scared to make new friends. My fear was that I'd get close to people and have to move again. But the fact that I spoke English and had lived in the U.S. made the kids in my grade like me. Also, I was letting everyone cheat off me during English tests, which probably helped. Suddenly everyone wanted to sit next to me. This got me invites to cool, coed birthday parties. For these parties, the kid's parents would always hire the same DJ, who went by the name of DJ Colacha. We were obsessed with DJ Colacha. The girls wanted to marry him, and the boys wanted to be him. He was twenty, had a ponytail, wore a brown leather vest with nothing under it, and he brought his own strobe light that was so potent that one time a boy named Hugo had a seizure that put him in the hospital for over a week. DJ Colacha also had this cool, original catchphrase that we all thought he totally came up with on his own, which he'd say into the microphone between songs, while grabbing his crotch. All the kids went crazy when he did that shit. You know what the catchphrase was? "Can't touch this!" But the highlight of these parties was when Colacha would play slow songs. That's when all the girls would line up in a row facing the boys, and we'd stand eight feet apart, swaying back and forth to sexy jams like "Nothing Compares 2 U," by Sinéad O'Connor.

Around this time, my parents forced me to start attending a Jewish club on Saturdays called Hebraica. It was more progressive than Dr. Herzl. We had counselors who were in their twenties and dressed cool, and they'd teach us about Judaism, but in fun ways. For example, they taught us how to make gnocchi and let us play basketball, which have no relation to Judaism whatsoever. But then they'd show us slideshows of Holocaust photos and tell us stories about how Hitler turned Jews into soap.

After one of these lessons, our counselor asked us to write down what we'd say to Hitler if we had the chance to tell him something. I told her that I wouldn't say anything to him. I'd just make him eat an entire baguette and a bag of potatoes without letting him drink water and then I'd bury him alive and build a mall on top of his body because he was "un sorete," a piece of shit. She told me violence was never the answer and that I shouldn't say the words *piece of shit* because it was bad manners.

Hebraica also hosted a year-end talent show in which every kid had to perform. When I heard about this, I begged my parents to let me skip it, but they refused. The thought of getting on that stage made me want to die. I wasn't going to embarrass myself and my family like I did after my last performance as a flower at Dr. Herzl. Even though I was in a better place and had come a long way from the days of dissociation, I still wasn't confident enough to sing and dance for a crowd full of people. Fuck that.

By then, the rabbits in my throat had cleared up. Now my emotional issues manifested themselves as unrelenting, chronic fevers. The first fever happened shortly after we moved back to Argentina, and it was caused by my watching an episode of *Beverly Hills 90210*. The song "Damn I Wish I Was Your Lover" played as Dylan and Kelly made out on some supercool Malibu beach. Meanwhile, here I was, lying on a mattress on the ground of my empty apartment in Argentina. That night, I cried myself to sleep and woke up with a fever of 102. Shortly after this, the fevers started happening all the time. I'd hear my parents argue about money and get a fever. I'd talk to Sandra on the phone (who had stayed in Northridge because she was going to marry her boyfriend, Mateo), and I'd get a fever.

The fevers would last four to five days, and they were so bad they made me hallucinate. Most of the hallucinations involved me being visited by God, who would float up to me and hover above my bed on a cloud. God was in his forties. He had a classic God look: white beard and a pretty good body with tons of muscles, which made me a little bit horny. He was a Hot God. During these visits, Hot God would assign me a very important task: to count every human who lived on Earth. I would then embark on this counting mission. I'd pick a country, count all its inhabitants, which usually went into the millions, then move on to the next country. Unfortunately, some of the people I had counted in certain countries ended up immigrating to different countries, so I'd have to start the count all over again. The thing was, I could never get the people on Earth to stop immigrating, at which point the impossibility and scale of my task would start to dawn on me, and I'd start to panic and scream like I was about to be murdered. My parents would usually wake me up when the screaming began, and I'd run to the bathroom and vomit uncontrollably.

These fevers happened over a dozen times in a single year. But there was one fever in particular that I'll never forget. It happened the week after the Hebraica talent show was announced. My issue with having to perform in the talent show wasn't just that I didn't want to be seen; it was that there was nothing I cared about enough to perform in front of a crowd full of people. The confident little girl who advertised Sexy Chicken door-to-door had fizzled away until the day when I awoke from my people-counting fever dream, completely drenched in sweat, and saw her face on TV for the first time. The woman who would forever change my life: Madonna Louise Veronica Ciccone.

The first thing I saw of hers was the music video for "La Isla Bonita." She was the most beautiful human being I had ever seen, wearing a red polka-dot flamenco dress and a huge flower in her hair. I was mesmerized. What drew me to Madonna wasn't just her looks or the way she sang. It was her intense gaze, which peered through the camera directly at me. It was also the fact that the song she was singing was in English and Spanish, and it was about an observer who desperately longed to be in a different place. A place that she constantly dreamed of that seemed *so far away*. That was exactly how I felt! It was that longing and that nostalgia that I felt for the

United States now that I lived in Argentina, as well as the longing and nostalgia I had felt for Argentina when I lived in the United States.

When the music video ended, I was desperate for more Madonna. I sat up in bed and prayed to Hot God. "Please God, I know I failed you with the counting of all the humans on Earth mission, but I beg you to give me more Madonna music videos." I wasn't one to pray to God. I had prayed only one other time in my life. But only because I was in desperate straits. It was a few years earlier, when we still lived in California and Pocho and Rita had taken me to Disneyland. After entering the park, Pocho walked directly into one of the gift shops on Main Street, put on a red baseball cap with an embroidered Mickey Mouse on it, and walked out of the store without paying for it. He was holding my hand the whole time, and I had totally noticed what he'd done. I was terrified. He was stealing something from the happiest place on Earth and that felt like the greatest crime one could ever commit. Plus, someone at school had told me that if you got caught doing crimes at Disneyland, you'd get put into Disneyland jail, where Goofy would torture you. And so, instead of enjoying the rides, I spent the entire day silently praying to God to not let us get arrested for stealing that hat. And guess what? The prayer worked, because Pocho never got caught. And on this day, God answered my prayer again, because when "La Isla Bonita" ended, a VJ with orange hair named Ruth appeared on the screen and announced that in honor of the release of Madonna's newest album, *Erotica*, MTV would be playing back-to-back Madonna music videos. *All. Day. Long.*

I was so enchanted, I didn't want to get up to go to the bathroom and forced myself to hold my pee the entire time.

Madonna's videos ranged from playful and fun, like the one for "Material Girl," where she wore an incredible fuchsia dress with opera gloves and snagged diamonds from men who swooned over her, to sexual ones like "Justify My Love," where she dragged herself across the floor of a hotel hallway and eventually stripped down from a black overcoat to a bra and a garter belt while rubbing her vagina.

I watched ten straight hours of Madonna music videos that day. When I finally made it to the bathroom, I caught a glimpse of myself in the mirror. I looked like absolute horse-shit. The fever had left me gaunt, with grayish skin, and huge bags under my eyes. But I stood there, staring at myself in that mirror, and knew something inside me was changing. Slowly, the expression on my face morphed. I cracked a small smile, which turned into a big Grinch-like grin. I then let out a maniacal laugh, as if I were a villain in a movie. Now that I knew Madonna existed, I felt confident again. I felt like a powerful diva. And I knew *exactly* what to do for the upcoming Hebraica talent show.

I decided that I wouldn't tell Mom or Dad what I'd be doing for the performance. I wanted it to be a surprise. They had patiently put up with an entire year of me acting like a wet noodle, so this was going to be a special gift from me to them. But that meant I'd have to enlist the help of an adult who could aid me in putting together a costume. By this time, my parents had moved Bubaleh out of Yiddishland and into my and my sister's playroom. Bubaleh now slept on a twin-size, pullout cot, surrounded by Barbies, Fisher-Price toys, and my poster of sexy Kevin Costner. Bubaleh didn't care, though. We were her new family, and she was the happiest person in the world.

The first step in preparing for the show was having Bubaleh walk me over to Musi Mundo, a record shop on Calle Corrientes. I sorted through the options and decided on Madonna's *The Immaculate Collection*, her first greatest hits album. The second, harder part, required Bubaleh's seamstress skills. Luckily, her sewing machine was one of the few belongings she had brought with her from Yiddish-land, along with her endless pictures of dead relatives, her cemetery, which she kept on a shelf next to our Mario and Luigi stuffed animals. The third and final step required her to find a specialty lingerie shop, which took a little more convincing.

Even though Hebraica was your average Jewish community center, its theater was the real deal. It sat over nine hundred people, had a state-of-the-art sound, lighting, and rigging system, an orchestra pit, and thick, red velvet curtains that slid across the stage and disappeared into the stage wings, where I waited for my name to be announced, watching the children who were performing before me. There was a little girl of about five with a speech impediment who recited a folkloric gaucho poem in blackface. I remember her crying because she didn't want to go onstage while her mother forcefully rubbed a piece of burnt cork all over her face. There was also a group of older girls doing Rikudim, a choreographed Jewish dance that involved them dancing around in circles, which caused their big breasts to flop around in the air and got them a standing ovation. And then it was my turn. The host looked at his cue cards and announced into the microphone: "And now, give a round of applause to Tamara Yajia." The theater went completely dark, and I walked onto center stage with no fear at all.

"Like a Prayer" begins with a simple electric guitar riff, which is followed by the sound of a prison door slamming shut. Before the show, I had instructed the lighting guy that that should be the cue for him to shine a single spotlight on me. He did so, revealing me on my knees, my hands clasped together in prayer position, with a black mole drawn above my lip, just like Madonna, and wearing one of Bubaleh's big black overcoats. Still on the ground, and with my eyes closed, I lip-synched the beginning of the song: *Life is a mystery . . .* I slowly crossed myself, just like I had seen Madonna do. Forehead, chest, left shoulder, then right shoulder. I then got on my feet, looked out onto the audience, and the first person I made eye contact with was Rabbi Isaac Groisman. He looked scared, and so did the two other rabbis in the audience. As the beat kicked in, I removed a small knife from the pocket of Bubaleh's coat and pretended to cut my hands with it, like Madonna did in the video. I then took off the coat and dramatically threw it across the stage. Underneath, I was wearing a big T-shirt, which belonged to my dad and went down to my knees. It had an American flag print on it. I lip-synched the lyrics "and it feels like home," realizing that I too felt at home again as I strutted across that stage, dancing to one of Madonna's most controversial and Catholic songs for a theater filled with moishes. I then crawled across the stage and rubbed my crotch, just like I'd seen Madonna rub hers in the "Like a Virgin" music video. I gave that crowd the performance of a fucking lifetime.

But the biggest surprise came at minute three of the song, when the choir begins singing *Just like a prayer, I'll take you there.* At that point, I stood center stage, grabbed the collar of my American flag shirt, and ripped it off just like strippers do in the movies, via a series of Velcro strips that Bubaleh had sewn onto the sides for me. The shirt tore off perfectly, like I had rehearsed it. And then I stood there under that spotlight. A nine-year-old wearing nothing but a garter belt, beige underwear that made me appear to be nude, and a tiny lace bralette, gazing out at an audience that looked like a truck was about to run them over, and I was the happiest I'd ever been in my entire life.

Ano Contra Natura

In January 1992, Nilda and Benjamín visited his oncologist to get the results of Benjamín's latest scan. The previous year, after he'd been diagnosed, Benjamín had gotten part of his colon removed. The surgery was successful, so Nilda threw a dinner party for thirty people to celebrate the fact that Grandpa would live. It was catered by El Ciervo de Oro (The Golden Stag), an iconic Jewish bakery in our neighborhood, which had been around for more than forty years. The bakery had been frequented by my parents, grandparents, *and* great-grandparents and went under during the Pandemic.

Some of the highlights from this party were as follows: There was a toddler who removed his diaper and sprayed piss all over Nilda's foyer after which she chased him around with a broom; I spent most of the evening looking through a pile of purses that the guests had left on Nilda's bed and found a toupee that smelled like a Bolognese sauce in one of them;

everyone was in excellent spirits about the fact that my grand-father had avoided getting an artificial anus, and all the adults kept repeating the phrase *ano contra natura*, which literally translates to anus against nature, over and over again. But the main highlight of the soiree was that my second cousin Damián, whom I was in love with ever since the day I was born, was there. I was nine and he was fifteen at the time, and I was always trying to give him kisses and sit on his lap like a horny little creep. (Many years later, when I was eighteen, I returned to Argentina for a different cousin's bar mitzvah where I bumped into Damián, who was now twenty-four. After the party ended, we got drunk together and he fingerbanged me in his car until a cop knocked on his window and asked me if I was "working" to which I answered, "No, we're cousins." I then gave him a twenty-dollar bill to leave us alone.)

Anyways, a few months after the celebratory party at Nilda's house, when she and Benjamín visited the oncologist for his latest scan result, the doctor informed them that, despite the fact that the tumor had been successfully removed from my grandfather's colon, the cancer had metastasized to his stomach and lungs. The prognosis was not good. This was a complete shock to the two of them, who had been celebrating his remission. After taking in his death sentence, my grandparents left the hospital in a daze and entered a taxi without saying a word to each other. "Where to?" asked the driver, who was wearing a top hat for some reason.

"Corner of Corrientes and Canning," answered Nilda. The strange driver began mimicking the motion of starting the car, except there was no key in the ignition. He made the sound "brooooom, brooooom" with his mouth, but the car didn't move, which my grandparents found odd, especially since the driver was pretending to move the steering wheel as if he were actually driving. At that moment, a hand holding a fly swatter came out from a hole in the back seat, hit the back of my grandpa's bald head, and quickly retracted into the hole. The mysterious hand came back out seconds later holding a yellow mustard bottle and squeezed a dollop of mustard on the top of my grandpa's head. It popped out again with a slice of tomato, some ham, and a slice of bread. It was making a sandwich of Grandpa!

Meanwhile, the driver kept on pretending to drive, making honking sounds with his mouth and complaining that the traffic was insane even though they hadn't moved an inch. Turns out there was a hidden camera in the taxi, and they were being filmed for one of Argentina's most famous TV prank shows.

Months later, as the cancer continued spreading into my grandpa's throat, causing him to constantly choke and spit out huge chunks of blood, we all went over to Nilda and Benjamín's apartment to watch this clip. We all lay in bed together watching Grandpa, on the worst day of his life, getting hit in the back of the head with that fly swatter, then turning around to look at what had touched him, and finding nothing, because the hand had quickly retreated into its hole. A true horror story.

Benjamín had not been the most present grandfather, especially when you compared him with Pocho. I was also raised with the notion that I'd disappointed him from day one, by being born a girl, a detail that my parents probably should never have told me. But after his cancer diagnosis, Benjamín began to take interest in me. After school, I started going over to his house, and we'd watch my favorite TV shows in his kitchen while he slurped on a cabbage and rice soup that he believed would cure his cancer, out of a bowl so large it resembled a bucket. When he was done with his soup, he'd clean out his teeth with a toothpick. He'd then examine the pick to see what hidden treasures he'd carved out from in between his molars and ended the ritual by giving the little sliver of wood a deep inhale so that he could take in the delightful and intoxicating scents that had emanated from his teeth. I never found this disgusting. It was Benjamín's toothpick-smelling ceremony. I found it to be beautiful. In the present day, I like to imitate him whenever I floss my teeth, and it's delightful.

One show that Benjamín and I watched was the infamous Argentine variety show for teenagers, *Jugate Conmigo*, which translates to something like "Play with Me." It was hosted by a thirty-something woman who wore pigtails. The show featured a group of ten super-hot teens, five of each sex, that sang songs about how they wanted to fuck each other really bad. I was totally in love with one of them. His name was Lucas, and he was fifteen years old, but to me he was a man. He was the goofy-slash-flirty one of the bunch, and he sang a song about having bad luck with girls. He was vulnerable, with puppy eyes, and brown curly hair. I had such a burning love for him that I would cry at night thinking about him. One day, my girlfriends even made a life-size cardboard cutout of him and brought him to school so that I could marry him during recess. He had a balloon for a head with a picture of Lucas's face taped to it that I passionately kissed after one of the girls in my grade pronounced us husband and wife. After the ceremony, I grabbed my new cardboard husband by the hand, and we performed a first dance while all the girls showered us with rice and made a complete mess of the playground, which almost got us suspended.

Benjamín could tell I was crushing hard on Lucas. Probably because I wouldn't shut the fuck up about him and kept referring to him as my *amor imposible*. One day we were watching TV in Benjamín's kitchen when he pulled out an envelope and handed it to me. "Let's go meet your *amor imposible*," he said. I tore the envelope open and found two tickets to see *Jugate Conmigo* live. I couldn't believe it! I hugged Benjamín as hard as I could. He smelled comforting, like chicken soup. And he was as thin as one of the toothpicks he used to clean his teeth with.

On March 17, 1992, while I got ready for Benjamín to pick me up for the big event, my parents came into my room to tell me that the show had been canceled. A half hour earlier, at 2:45 P.M., a Ford F-100, packed with explosives, driven by a suicide bomber, had crashed through the front of the Israeli Embassy in Buenos Aires, leaving the city completely paralyzed. "And what does that have to do with the *Jugate Conmigo* show?" I asked, filling up with rage.

"A lot of people died today, Tamara," Dad explained.

"How many people? A million?" I answered. I needed at least a million deaths to justify the *Jugate Conmigo* show getting canceled. What a little bitch I was.

"Listen to me, you selfish little shit," Mom interjected. "People died. The show is canceled, and that's that." I lost my goddamn mind.

"I don't care about the dead. I want to go see *Jugate Conmigo* with Grandpa. I want to marry Lucas. I hate you both. I hate life!" I screamed and kicked, eventually slamming the door to my room on my parents' faces, which got me grounded for a week.

A few months later, all the kids in my grade were put on a school bus, and we were taken on a morbid field trip to see the remains of the destroyed embassy. The bus parked across the street, and we sat in silence looking out the window at the debris, which made me feel kind of guilty for saying I didn't care about the dead; I felt like Hot God was going to punish me soon for being a selfish little shit. When school got out, my parents picked me up and told me Benjamín had passed. "It's my fault he died," I told them. "I'm being punished for not caring about the dead. And I'm probably going to die next."

My parents didn't let me attend Benjamín's funeral because they felt that I was too young and also because I'd become obsessed with dying and death. Instead, Pocho and Rita took me for ice cream and then to the movies to see *Schindler's List*. Unbelievable. But get this, as the three of us entered the movie theater, I looked to my right and there he was, sitting just a few seats over from me: my love, my *amorsito*, Lucas. I immediately told Pocho that sitting near us was my *amor imposible*, the man I wanted to marry. "Which one is he?" asked Pocho. I pointed at Lucas, who was wearing a white turtleneck and sitting with two people I assumed were his parents. "The one with the giant schnozzola that looks like an eggplant?!" answered Pocho, in a voice that was way too loud for my comfort. (For the record, Lucas did *not* have a giant schnozzola that looked like an eggplant.) Regardless, Pocho grabbed me by the hand. "Let's go meet him," he said and walked me over to Lucas. "I'm sorry to bother you," said Pocho, "but my granddaughter is a big fan, and she's very sad because her other grandfather is being buried today." Lucas looked at me with his puppy eyes, and he looked genuinely sad for me.

"What's your name?" he asked, while caressing my fucking cheek!

"Tamara," I answered, completely frozen in disbelief that this was happening.

"I love you, Tamara," Lucas said, then planted a luscious, wet kiss on my cheek. I refused to wash my face for the next month. Lucas is now a psychiatrist who focuses on anxiety and depression.

The Voice of a Penis

My "Like a Prayer" performance was a major turning point in my life, and I'll get into what came of it in just a moment. But first, I need to explain something about my family, namely, that my parents were *not* appalled that, as a preteen, I stripped down to lingerie in front of a theater packed with adults and rabbis. On the contrary, my parents fucking *loved* it.

The human body was never a taboo in my family. As a matter of fact, crass subjects such as sex and defecation were totally normal for us. The thing is that the parameters for what was okay and not okay to discuss were weird, shifty, and unpredictable. For example, I wasn't allowed to watch *The Simpsons* because there was burping in it, which my parents found disgusting. Farts were also considered vulgar, and they didn't like me ripping any in front of them. At the same time, though, they were totally fine with us talking about the consistency of our bowel movements while we sat at the dinner table. So, in review: farts and burps were a no, but shit was celebrated. This remains true to the present day; on most days I could tell you whether Dad has diarrhea or if Mom is constipated. This was true of my grandparents as well. One day Rita complained to Mom and Dad about how terribly constipated she was. Dad jokingly advised her to put on a pair of gloves and dig out the poop from her ass with her fingers. She called him the next day to thank him for his guidance.

"I didn't have gloves, so I wrapped my hand in a supermarket bag," she told Dad. "But your trick worked perfectly."

Sexuality was another subject that was openly discussed in detail and without shame. There were positive aspects to this, like the time I was eleven and walked into the bathroom while Mom was taking a bath to ask her what oral sex was. (I had overheard an older girl in school tell her friends that you most likely wouldn't get pregnant from oral sex.) Mom, who was wearing a shower cap and shaving her toes, told me that oral sex was when "people lick, and suck, each other's penises and vaginas." She then added, "It feels great, and me and your dad do it a couple of times a week because we love each other."

There were also admittedly situations in which this openness was borderline inappropriate. Actually, straight-up inappropriate. Like when, during Passover dinner, Pocho told the table a "fairy tale" (these were his words) about a princess in a faraway land who was so dissatisfied with the penis sizes of all the townsmen that she procured a donkey. While devouring a chunk of gefilte fish with his mouth open, he went into further detail about the mechanism of the story, explaining that the maiden would "wrap a towel around the donkey's penis and let it fuck her." What's insane about all of this to me is that the only part of that story that my eleven-year-old brain found disturbing, unnecessary, and hard to believe was that the maiden needed to wrap the donkey's penis in a towel in order to have sex with it. I still can't figure out what the purpose of the towel was. Was she afraid to raw dog it? Was the towel some sort of birth control? I guess I'll never know.

This trait didn't exist only on Mom's side of the family. During Benjamín's final years, our favorite activity was to drive as a family to Buenos Aires's red-light district, where men would go to pick up prostitutes. Mom, Dad, my sister, and I would pile into the back of Nilda's car, and she'd drive us up and down the street so we could marvel at the semi-nude bodies of these statuesque women. During these drives, I'd press my face against the back window of the car and wave at the gorgeous creatures who displayed themselves for their clientele, wearing nothing but G-strings and high heels. Most of them would wave back and blow kisses at me, which made me feel cool. But once one of the prostitutes, who was wearing a skin-tight leopard catsuit with two holes in the back, from which her perfectly round ass cheeks popped out, walked up to our car and yelled "get your fucking children out of here, you psychos." Enraged, Nilda stuck her head out the window:

"Chupame un huevo hija de puta," Grandma yelled back at the woman. This is a famous Argentine expression that literally translates to "suck one of my nuts, you bitch."

So no, me being in a garter belt, pretending to masturbate for a crowd of nine hundred people, wasn't horrifying for my parents in the least. In fact, they knew they had a star on their hands. After the talent show, I was enrolled in as many dancing, singing, and acting classes as I could fit into my schedule. There was the beginners' step-aerobics class, which I mastered so quickly that I was bumped up to the advanced level. I was a little twerp, with spaghetti-like arms and legs, and no boobs, dancing in a neon leotard alongside grown-ass women who had curves, periods, pubic hair, and wild body odor that smelled like fried onions.

There were also my short-lived acting classes taught by an old, gay thespian who wore a beret and smoked four packs of cigarettes a day. No, I am not exaggerating. His teeth were the color of sewer water, and, I swear to god, he looked like he was dying of every disease that has ever existed. As a warm-up, he'd turn the theater lights off and make us walk around in the dark. Whenever he turned the lights back on, we'd have to insult whichever student was nearest to us. The first time we did this horrifying exercise, the kids uttered classic and generic insults at each other like "you're ugly" or "you smell like rotten eggs." When it was my turn to spew my venom, however, I drew a blank, then, to the sweet young girl with pigtails who stood before me, blurted out, "You're a rapist." The second time we did the insult exercise, our elderly teacher turned the lights off, and he never turned them back on, because he went into diabetic shock.

In place of my defunct acting class, my parents were advised to send me to train with the amazing Conchita Lorenzo. On top of being a character straight out of a Pedro Almodóvar movie, Conchita was a vocal instructor, choreographer, *and* manager for child performers. Conchita was from Spain, where the name Conchita (short for Concepción) is totally normal and common. In Argentina, *conchita* is also common, but in a different way. It is slang for "little vagina." If you were to Google *conchita*, you'd notice that it appears in numerous articles with titles like "Everyday Spanish Words You Want to Avoid While Visiting Argentina."

Conchita was no taller than five feet and had the physique of a bodybuilder. When she wasn't moving, she kind of resembled one of the tough, axe-wielding Dwarves from *Lord of the Rings*. But the moment that woman started dancing, the moment she raised one of her legs in the air and pointed her toes, she turned into a fucking gazelle. I once overheard one kid's father say, "I want Conchita to fuck me and then kick the living shit out of me."

Not only was Conchita talented, she was able to recognize talent. She accepted only the most gifted children into her studio. And she didn't just take actors or singers. Among her pupils was Fede, a twelve-year-old juggler who dreamed of being a famous clown one day. When I met him, I was convinced that one day he'd be my husband. Fede lived in one of Buenos Aires's Villa Miserias, the dangerous shantytowns whose residences were mostly shacks made out of tin, wood, or other scrap material. Conchita discovered him when she pulled up to a red light and saw him juggling Fanta bottles on the sidewalk, asking drivers for spare change. Fede's other talent was that he could eat paper, which Conchita could *not fucking stand*. "That isn't a talent, Fede," she said to him once, "it's a cry for goddamn help." Conchita banned him from eating paper if he was in her presence. One time, however, I did catch Fede, staring out the window, contemplating life in a position that resembled Rodin's *The Thinker*, while crumpling up pieces of ruled school paper into balls and swallowing them whole. He was so beautiful. I gathered all the courage I had and walked up to him ready to pop the big question. "Hi, Fede. Do you want to be my husband or my boyfriend?" I asked.

"No," he answered, while still looking out the window. He then crumpled a piece of paper into a ball, put it in his mouth, and swallowed it dramatically. "I don't have time for love. I'm trying to be the world's greatest juggling clown."

"Fine," I replied. "But you should stop eating paper. You're going to give your turds paper cuts." He didn't find this funny, but he did end up becoming a successful juggling clown as an adult and today travels the world performing his art for people.

Another notable character from Conchita's studio was Cecilia, a girl my age who couldn't sing, act, or dance for shit. Cecilia's sole talent was her striking beauty, which, for that reason and that reason alone, enabled her to never stop booking TV commercials. I was jealous of Cecilia and gave her the stink-eye every time she looked my way. What made it worse was that she made a ton of money from her commercials even though she didn't need it because her parents were already rich. I hated how easily things came for her. Cecilia's perfect presence was so unforgivable to me that I got revenge on her by spreading a rumor that she was adopted.

The weirdest of all the people at Conchita's studio, though, was a man who went by the name "Lord Chaos." Chaos, as we called him, was Conchita's only employee. He was a goth dude in his forties who never spoke and scared the crap out of me. He always wore black and had dark hair down to his waist. Lord Chaos, whose name I wound up learning was actually Juan Lopez, was a producer and music engineer whose job was to record those of us who were singers. Since there wasn't much space in Conchita's studio, however, Chaos had set up a makeshift recording booth inside a utility closet, where we sang surrounded by brooms, buckets, and cans of Raid.

The day I met Conchita, she was sitting in a folding chair, near one of her studio's giant windows. There was a sunbeam illuminating her, which made her look like a goddess to me. That day, I auditioned for her by doing my Madonna routine. I was so in the zone that I didn't even notice that my bralette had slipped, and I performed the majority of the routine with my nipples hanging out. But I immediately became her number one.

Conchita had a concrete plan for me: I was to become a pop star. I was only eleven, which she felt was a bit young. "The ideal age for a pop star is fifteen or sixteen," Conchita told me after our first meeting. "And the Madonna striptease is too much. I love it. But it's too much. No one wants to see a child dancing around with her twat hanging out."

"I *like* the Madonna striptease," I answered, standing my ground.

"Fine, you can keep doing it every now and then, but it shouldn't be your bread and butter. And I want sound coming out of your mouth, Tamara. Lip-syncing is for peasants." I agreed. Something about the way this strong woman spoke to me made me feel like I was an intelligent adult, like my opinions mattered.

That same day we began singing lessons. My voice was a bit of a mess at first; there was a squeaky quality to it that made me sound like a chipmunk. In Argentina there's an expression for this kind of annoying, high-pitched voice. We call it *voz de pito*, which translates to "voice of a penis." According to Conchita, I had the *voice of a penis*. To correct this, she made me strengthen my diaphragm by teaching me an exercise in which I repeatedly blew on a feather, to keep it from touching the ground. She also helped me lower my register by making me sing the song "Mmm Mmm Mmm Mmm," by the Crash Test Dummies, over and over and over again, which I'm certain forever altered my voice. This incredibly dark song, which tells the story of various lonely children who suffer from physical abnormalities, is so reminiscent of my childhood and so indicative of that wonderful time in my life (my *favorite* time in my life) that whenever I hear it, I can't help but get full body chills. What I'm about to admit is very weird, but, not long ago, I heard the song while driving, and the singer's low, bassy voice caused me to have an orgasm without touching myself and almost crash into the freeway's center divider.

After a few singing lessons, Conchita had Lord Chaos record a tape of me singing "All That She Wants," by Ace of Base, inside his utility closet. I picked this song not only because of its popularity at the time but because it was easy to sing. I also liked that it was about a powerful woman who did whatever the fuck she wanted. Just like Conchita, the song made me feel empowered. Once we had that sample, she began submitting me to various events in and around Buenos Aires.

Almost immediately, I began getting booked at festivals like the Feria de la Rural, Buenos Aires's biggest county fair, in which you could ride carnival rides, enjoy musical acts like mine, and pet some of Argentina's most prestigious breeds of cows. Soon enough, I was performing every single weekend. Some of the songs in my repertoire were "All That She Wants," of course, as well as Ace of Base's other hit, "The Sign," which was a little harder but always made the crowd go nuts. I'd also alternate between "La Isla Bonita" and "Cherish," by Madonna, and throw in a few songs in Spanish like "Desesperada," by Marta Sánchez, and another song in which Fede the juggler would join me onstage for an unacceptably bad rap cameo that he would always fumble. "Some people should stick to their skills," I complained to Conchita once. She agreed and never let Fede hold a microphone again. I'd sing all these songs live, like a total pro, using a fancy, wireless microphone that Pocho bought me for my birthday. Whenever I arrived at a gig, the sound engineer would hand me the generic microphone that came with the stage, and I'd say, "No thanks. I'll be using my own," like the little diva that I was.

For two years, I performed at art fairs, sporting events, benefits for abused elders, and schools for disabled children, whom I'd always invite onstage to dance with me. Once, during a performance at an association for people with Down syndrome, I invited a teenage boy to get onstage with me. Before I knew it, dozens of kids were climbing on that makeshift stage and trying to rip the microphone out of my hands. So many people climbed on that one of the wooden boards cracked, and the entire stage collapsed. One guy broke his wrist! After that, I never invited anyone to dance onstage with me again.

But seriously, I couldn't begin to list all the random-ass places I performed. What I *could* tell you is that I fucking loved doing it. I loved singing and dancing so much that I even did it when I wasn't getting booked to do it. One year my parents and I vacationed in Miramar, a coastal town that's about five hours outside Buenos Aires. During the day, we'd go to a beach club that had a bar and was always packed with people.

I noticed the bar had a PA system that could be heard throughout the entire beach. So, the next day, when we returned to the beach, I brought the tape of me singing "All That She Wants," which Lord Chaos had recorded. Without telling my parents, I walked up to the bar and asked them if they'd announce on their PA that there would be a special performance at 3 P.M. sharp. They agreed, no questions asked. I then taught my sister, who was only seven at the time, a simple choreography so that she could act as my backup dancer. That day, about sixty people flocked to the bar to see me perform "All That She Wants" in a two-piece, skimpy, tie-dye bathing suit.

To be clear, neither Conchita nor my parents ever forced me to perform. Not once. Sure, Conchita booked all my shows and helped me polish my act, but I was my own creative director. I was the Don Draper of my child star career. I choreographed my own routines and made sketches of what outfits I wanted to wear so that Bubaleh could design them for me. Among my most memorable costumes were the cutoff denim shorts that exposed the bottom half of my butt cheeks, and the black, vinyl miniskirt that I wore with Dr. Martens and thigh highs, a tight silver top, and a black velvet hat. These were less provocative than the garter belt costume, which I eventually phased out, but they were still a lot for a little girl. Which leads me to my next point: There is absolutely *no doubt* that I was one-hundred-percent sexualized as a child.

The first time it happened was after my Hebraica performance, when I was nine. My group and I had gone on a field trip to the Jewish Museum of Buenos Aires, and I was standing in front of a painting that had captivated my attention. It was titled *The Immigrants*, and it depicted a family about to embark on a boat ride in order to emigrate from Poland to Argentina. Everyone in the painting looked so bummed out, especially the children. It was a total depression. Their expressions reminded me of how I felt when we returned to Buenos Aires. As I stood there, a boy from my group walked up to me and whispered in my ear. "I liked your dancing, little slut. How much do you charge per hour?" I could tell by his breath that he had a cavity in one of his teeth. Despite this upsetting stench of rot, I blushed and laughed. I actually felt kind of flattered by his comment. That's because I focused only on the "I liked your dancing part" of it. But later that night as I was lying in bed, the rest of his comment popped into my head. The "little slut" part. The "How much do you charge per hour" part. The more I thought about what this sick little fuck said to me, the more confused I got. Was he kidding or did he really want to pay me by the hour? I knew men paid for prostitutes by the hour, of course. I was familiar with prostitutes from our family outings. I loved them, and sex work wasn't some taboo thing to me. But was I a prostitute too? And what did it mean to be a little slut? Was it bad to be a little slut? It's weird because, in the present, when I talk about my child star days, the first thing I tell people was that I danced around stages dressed like a "little slut." I don't lead with the fact that I was a talented, creative child, or a great dancer. That description of myself has stuck with me ever since.

On another occasion, after a show, I was approached by a pretty cute guy of about seventeen. My parents must have still been standing in the crowd when this teenager cornered me and told me how pretty I was. I was chewing gum at the time, and he held his hand out to me and said, "Let me have your gum." I offered him a fresh piece, but that's not what he wanted. "Give me the one that's in your mouth," he said. I wanted to run away, but I figured the polite, and easiest, thing to do was to just give it to him. So I spit out my prechewed slimy-ass gum in his big, calloused hand. He put it in his mouth and started savoring it in a very intense way. He was moaning. His eyes were rolling to the back of his head and shit. "Thank you for that," he said. He wanted to keep talking, but I told him I had to leave and headed back into my dressing room where I sat in silence trying to process what had just happened. I was mostly confused, but it also felt . . . kind of good? I don't know. I felt powerful knowing that a cute older guy was desperate to eat gum straight out of my mouth. It also made me horny. But in a bad, guilty kind of way.

One New Year's Eve I performed in a venue outside Buenos Aires. The entire time I was onstage, I noticed a balding man in his fifties standing in the front row. You know what he was doing? He was looking up my skirt. He was examining me in such a creepy, violating way that I wanted to stop the show and cry out for my mom. All the moisture in my mouth disappeared. My mouth suddenly became so dry that my upper lip stuck to my teeth. I looked like Fire Marshal Bill. I sucked it up and completed the show. But when I got offstage, I saw him walking toward me, smoking a cigarette. I wanted to scream for help. But I thought, "Don't make a big deal. What if he's a nice, regular man and you embarrass him?" His feelings were more important than mine. When he approached me, he stopped, took the cigarette out of his mouth, and put it out on my arm, completely burning my flesh. Then he kept walking, and I never saw him again. I was in so much shock that I didn't even feel the burn at first. I walked out into the audience to where Conchita was sitting and showed her my arm. When she asked me what happened, I said, "A man burned me with his cigarette by mistake." By mistake, my ass. I knew that sick fuck burned me on purpose. And I knew he enjoyed it too. He had the same look on his face that the teenage boy had when he stuck my gum in his mouth. The worst, worst, WORST part about this was that later that night, even though my arm throbbed from pain, I was once again flooded with that weird, bad, horny feeling.

I have to admit, of all these horrifying incidents, the one that got to me the most happened at home and had nothing to do with performing. I was riding the elevator up to our apartment with Mom and Dad, and raving about how much I loved one of my teachers at Hebraica. His name was Sebastian, and he was in his thirties. He was the best. In a non-creepy way. "Sebastian told me there's gonna be a camp coming up and we'll get to build our own tents!" I told them as the elevator went up. "Sebastian taught me how to serve a volleyball without having my wrist hurt." And then as we reached our floor and I opened the elevator door, I overheard Dad whisper something to Mom that I probably wasn't supposed to hear, and that I wish I'd never heard.

"Sebastian probably wants to fuck her," he told her.

Something changed for me after that. The fact that these men wanted me was being validated, and not by just anyone, but by my own father. The boy who called me a slut, the teenager with the gum, the man with the cigarette. All of them wanted to fuck me. From that day on, there was a heaviness that followed me around. I became hyperaware of the presence of grown men and how they looked at me, whether it was a family friend or a man sitting at a restaurant with his family. I started paying attention to men, locking eyes with them at public places. And it became a compulsion. I couldn't not look at them. At one point, I even stopped worrying about the men who *did* look at me sexually and became concerned with those who *didn't* look at me from across the room. I would get upset if I failed to attract an older man. Like I hadn't done my job. I never told anyone about any of this. Until now, I guess.

My sexualization didn't stop me from wanting to perform, however. That's how much I loved it, and I was soon discovered by a talent agent who had me take professional headshots. For the pictures, Dad flat-ironed my long, brown hair by placing my head over a table and using a clothing iron. I looked adorable, posing in a black turtleneck and a hat with a huge sunflower on it by a tree at a park. After that, I embarked on the hell that is the world of auditioning. I auditioned for a brand that made soup for diabetic kids, in which I had to pretend to be happy and dance with a boy my age, but I screwed up by accidentally smacking him right on the penis while waving my hands during a twirl, causing him to drop to the ground in pain. There was a toothpaste commercial in which I had to pretend that something was really funny, which resulted in me being scolded by the casting agent for "covering my mouth" while I laughed.

At first, I wasn't booking shit. I straight-up wasn't made like the other smiley, normal kids I auditioned with. They were moldable, plain, and acted like children. I, on the other hand, exuded a sexuality, a darkness, an intensity that was too much for soup commercials. This intensity could be attributed to various factors. One was the fact that I had been modeling myself after Madonna. The other was that I'd started to perceive myself as a sexual being at such a young age. Regardless, commercials weren't for me.

My luck changed right as I was about to give up. Conchita signed me up to audition for *Nubeluz*, a Peruvian TV show for kids that I used to watch with Benjamín and dreamed of being on. The show was coming to Argentina for a couple of weeks and would be televised from the Gran Rex, a theater built in 1937 and designed to resemble Radio City Music Hall. People like Bob Dylan, Duke Ellington, and Cyndi Lauper performed there, and now there I was doing choreography, dressed in a golden jumpsuit with clouds on it, singing backup vocals on a song about how parents shouldn't smoke cigarettes because it makes their breath smell bad and causes them to die an agonizing early death from cancer. I was even asked to sign autographs after the show! I wasn't just yet the pop star Conchita had hoped I'd be. But I was on my way, kind of.

After the *Nubeluz* show, my agent sent me to what she referred to as a "very important audition." Mom accompanied me to this big loft with exposed brick, where I was given twenty minutes to memorize a song about the environment. It went something like "Baby, won't you help me save the Earth? Baby, please. I want plants and trees in this world for me and you, baby." I thought the song was an absolute cheese, but I still put on my sunflower hat and sang it for a panel of five serious adults who looked important. After I was done with my razzle-dazzle, they thanked me for my time, and I forgot about it.

Three weeks later, I was sitting at my kitchen table, eating a boiled hot dog that Mom had made for me, when my phone rang. My agent was on the other end. She asked me to get my parents. I had them pick up their bedroom line while I secretly listened from the kitchen. The agent told Mom that I had been selected from thousands of children to be a part of Argentina's answer to the Mickey Mouse Club (a bootleg, unofficial, version, that is). I was, in fact, being offered the lead role by the producer. And this wasn't just any producer, it was Argentina's biggest producer. This gig was way bigger than any state fair or toothpaste commercial; this was the real deal. I would be starring on a TV show that aired Monday through Friday and would go on hiatus for only a few months a year, during which we would travel around the country doing live shows. I would obviously be well compensated, but it would require me to be taken out of fifth grade and be homeschooled. It was everything I ever wanted. I was fucking jumping for joy while covering my mouth so that my parents didn't know I was listening. Then, I heard them tell the agent something that left me so shocked I let the phone slip from my hands and fall to the floor, like in the movies. "Tamara won't be able to take that job," said Mom, lowering her voice to make sure I didn't hear this from the other room. "We haven't told her yet, but we have decided to leave Argentina and return to the United States."

The President Is a Ball Sack
with Sideburns

The year leading up to the phone call from my agent, a call that should have brought me the best news in the world but ended up being one of the most devastating moments of my life (even worse than having my flesh burned with a cigarette by a pedophile), was a financially disastrous year for my parents. As consumed as I'd been by performing and becoming a pop icon, I still knew something bad was up.

When we initially returned to Argentina and Dad joined Benjamín's textile business, we actually enjoyed a good couple of financial years. It was one of those rare moments in my life when a large chunk of my brain wasn't preoccupied with worrying about my parents not having enough money. We moved to a nice doorman building where Mom hadn't made enemies of every single neighbor by leaving passive-aggressive notes in the lobby. Our new apartment was huge, with shiny marble floors, and a long wraparound balcony (with floor-to-ceiling metal bars that made it look like a prison, but whatever), from which I'd spit down on passersby. Mom and I would lie out on that balcony and tan during the scorching, ninety-five-degree Buenos Aires summers and squirt each other with spray bottles to cool ourselves off. We even helped Bubaleh with the down payment on a small apartment a block away from us, from where she'd operate her own clothing alterations business. Finally, at seventy-six, Bubaleh was independent and thriving. She even told people to stop calling her Bubaleh and start referring to her as "Rosa," because she felt that it made her sound more elegant and mysterious and would help her attract more customers and maybe even a boyfriend.

After years of borrowing Nilda's car, we were able to afford our own. A light blue Volkswagen Golf that had built-in defrosters in the back window, which allowed Dad to simply press a button to get rid of the frost instead of manually having to scrape it every morning. I couldn't tell you why, but this simple little comfort of having built-in defrosters made me feel rich and powerful. Like we had entered a new elite social status. As a matter of fact, I wouldn't shut up about the defrosters. I even did a presentation about them for science class, and dedicated pages in my diaries to discussing them and making detailed drawings of them. I guess we can't control the things we fall in love with. For me, it was Madonna and window defrosters.

It was during this prosperous time that Mom and Dad took me out of Dr. Hertzl and enrolled me in Lange Ley, an expensive private English-language school I loved. Here I was required to wear a uniform consisting of a pleated skirt, a crisp, button-up shirt with a tie, and a navy blue blazer. My parents also got me retainers to correct my giant middle teeth (which had started drifting in opposite directions and made me look like the guy from the cover of *Mad* magazine). But the best part of having that extra sweet, sweet cash was that we were able to afford an appearance by DJ Colacha for my eleventh birthday party. Mom and Dad even paid an extra fee for the "Deluxe Experience." This meant Colacha would stay for an extra hour and play older songs for the adults, which would always end in a conga line. He played songs by Julio Iglesias, Lionel Richie, and the Bee Gees. I guess this luxury was more for my parents than for me, but the party was still a hit, and I looked cool as fuck. I wore a western-inspired outfit with white cowboy boots and a fringe leather vest. I looked so damn good that day that, during a slow dance, Rodrigo, the tallest and most desired boy in my grade, asked me to be his girlfriend. "I don't think so," I answered, because having a boyfriend meant I was one step closer to getting married, and getting married meant that I'd have to bear children, and then what would happen? My parents would die, obviously. I was *not* ready for all of that shit. After going down this existential spiral and turning Rodrigo down, I was so overcome with the desire to be a baby and drink milk from my mother's teat that, when the song ended, I let go of his shoulders, locked myself in the bathroom, and cried.

We were even able to travel outside the country and vacation in our favorite place, Rio de Janeiro. A few days prior to our departure, Mom made the fatal mistake of sharing our flight and hotel information with Pocho. When Mom, Dad, my sister, and I boarded the plane, we heard someone yell "Surprise!" and realized that Pocho and Rita were sitting right behind us wearing matching floral shirts. Dad looked like someone punched him right in the stomach. By this time, Dad had become more defiant of his father-in-law. He no longer worked for him and made money of his own. So the entire vacation he argued with Pocho over everything: from who was a better tipper and more liked by the hotel staff, to who could take the longest piss. I'm serious. Once, Pocho pulled our rental car over in the middle of a bridge near Copacabana because he had to piss. Dad followed him out and they pulled their pants down and had a showdown, simultaneously urinating in the Atlantic Ocean. Pocho won. A few days later, I ate too many papayas and got diarrhea as we were crossing that exact same bridge, so I dangled my ass out the side and shat in the Atlantic Ocean. This diarrhea story has nothing to do with Pocho and Dad's relationship, or with my family having a few years of good fortune, but I wanted to mention it anyway because defecating directly into the ocean made me feel free.

But as it usually goes for us, our good fortune came to an end not long after it began. A few months following Benjamín's death, there was a dip in the economy, and his textile business, which Dad had taken over, went bankrupt, leaving Dad jobless and broke. The first sign that the money was dwindling was that, at Lange Ley, I could no longer eat the fixed-lunch menu like the other kids. Instead, Mom started sending me to school with Tupperware full of leftovers like beef stew from last night's dinner. For a few weeks, I continued sitting at the regular table with the other kids, and the kitchen staff was nice enough to heat up my Tupperware in the microwave, so I wouldn't have to eat my lunch cold. But not long after, the school was bought by a new owner who was cheap. When he got word that the kitchen staff was heating up my food for free, he made them stop. Not only was I forced to eat my food cold after that, but they actually separated me from the kids whose parents paid for lunch (which was all of them) and made me eat at a table by myself.

School lunches weren't the only cutbacks, of course. In the mid-nineties it was in style for kids who wore retainers to have these plastic, neon containers that hung around their necks in which they could store their mouthpieces while they ate. They were all the rage, at least in Argentina. They were status symbols. My parents had bought me one during our glory days. Unfortunately, I had the annoying habit of opening and closing mine nonstop because the sound of the plastic clicking was soothing and calmed me down. Eventually, I opened and closed the thing so much that the container snapped and broke. Since Mom and Dad couldn't afford a new one, Dad drilled two holes into a medium-size Tupperware, put a string through it, and hung that around my neck as a replacement retainer container.

Eventually, I was taken out of Lange Ley because no money was coming in and we were using our savings to pay for basics like food and rent. Before enrolling me in a public school, though, my parents had me take an admissions test at one of Buenos Aires's most respected schools that specialized in languages, specifically English and French. It was a *very* expensive school that was reserved for the children of ambassadors and diplomats, but gave a handful of scholarships to a few gifted, poor students every year. (I later found out that, during the dictatorship, this school was attended by the children of all the high-ranking fascists.) To prepare for the test, I was given a binder full of material that I had a week to study. I was so pissed off about having to switch schools again that I decided not to study a damn thing. I didn't care what school I went to anymore. My parents could enroll me in a school for farm animals, and I'd be fine with it. Instead of preparing, I spent the entire day watching *Jem and the Holograms*, reading an unauthorized Madonna biography, and eating sweet puffed corn. The day before the test, I put the binder they gave me under my pillow in the hope that the information would seep into my head, magically. The next morning, when the test was placed in front of me, I was so checked out, I didn't even fully read the prompts. A few days later, we were informed that not only had I been admitted to this school, but I would be bumped up a whole grade. I'd like to give myself the credit and think that I'm truly gifted, but I think the pages from the binder really did seep into my brain overnight.

Dr. Hertzl was made up of only Jewish kids, and Lange Ley was half-and-half. In this new school, I was the only Jew. Actually, that's not true. There was one girl named Jenny in my class with a Jewish last name. During my first week, I ran up to her at recess and excitedly said, "You're Jewish, right?"

"Yeah, but I don't like to share that with the kids in this school," she whispered back. To me this was pretty weird. I didn't understand until, one day, at a birthday party, we were told to get into teams and pick a team name. One of the boys, a rich, prepubescent dildo, suggested that his team be called "The Nazis." I had to hold back tears for the remainder of that party; all I could think about was the fact that I'd been taught at Hebraica about how Nazis turned people into soap. After that, I started noticing that most of the boys in my class were drawing little swastikas on the palms of their hands and in their notebooks, and carving them into trees. I took Jenny's advice and never mentioned that I was Jewish again.

Dad tried manufacturing children's clothing, which he'd sell door-to-door at brick-and-mortar shops. He made a few sales, but most of the checks bounced, and he found himself losing time and money. Eventually, his only source of income was attending these product-testing sessions, which paid the equivalent of five or ten dollars for him to drive across town, sit in a room full of other unemployed people, and give his opinion on the latest potato chip flavor.

It wasn't just my parents. All their friends struggled too. The entire middle class was collapsing. Couples were moving back in with their parents, taking their kids out of private schools, or straight up leaving the country. Instead of going out to eat on weekends, my parents' friends started gathering in our apartment. Together, they cooked a big pot of tripe soup that everyone pitched in on. They chain-smoked cheap cigarettes all night while complaining about the president, Carlos Menem, and about how miserable their lives were. (I heard them talk so much shit about Menem during that time that at school, I once referred to him as a "ball sack with sideburns." I got suspended for a day and was forced to write an apology letter to him, which was absolute bullshit because the truth is, all politics aside, he did look like a ball sack with sideburns.) During those gatherings, I'd lie in bed surrounded by the stench of tobacco, eating sweet puffed corn (I was really into sweet puffed corn during this phase of my life), half-listening to my parents complain, half-watching a VHS full of tracking lines of Jim Carrey's *The Mask*, wishing that I too would come across a psychotic, magical mask that helped me solve all my problems.

Once our savings ran out, we had to resort to selling our belongings. I said goodbye to my precious window defrosters when we got rid of our car, and we sold anything that wasn't of basic use: our blender, our VHS camera, the TV that we kept in the kitchen. We stopped buying anything unless it was absolutely essential, and we ate a lot of boiled hot dogs and rice. There was a time my class took a field trip to see the exhibit of my favorite painter, Fernando Botero. I had to skip out on this event because my parents couldn't afford to pay my museum entrance fee. I was obsessed with Botero's chunky men and women, and wanted to see those paintings so bad that I snapped at Dad and told him to "go out and get a job." Mom was so appalled at what I'd said to Dad that she smacked me across the face so hard I can still feel it burn.

This all brings me back to the day when my agent called to inform my parents that I had been cast in what would turn out to be one of Argentina's biggest TV shows. After they got off the phone, I ran into their room in such a hysterical state (not only because they had just turned down the role I'd been dreaming of, but because I had found out we were leaving Argentina, again) that they had to restrain me and throw me in a cold shower with my clothes on until I calmed down. The next day, I took a pair of scissors and cut my beautiful long hair off. I looked like the survivor of a clown holocaust. I had long strands, short strands, and a few patches of almost baldness throughout. I looked so embarrassing that Pocho took me to a salon to get it fixed because my parents couldn't afford to. The hairdresser gave me a messy, nineties Jennifer Aniston–layered look that left me looking like a wet rat.

Pocho and Rita weren't spared by the economy either. Pocho's import toy business started doing so shitty that they had to give up their flat and move into a run-down apartment full of leaks and moldy ceilings in the hectic garment district.

They lived there rent-free because the place belonged to Rita's cousin, my extravagant, millionaire great-aunt Chichi.

Chichi was the richest person in my extended family. She never married and dedicated her life to building one of Argentina's biggest transportation companies, a company as big as FedEx in the United States. Rita haaaaaated Chichi. Mostly because she was jealous of how rich she was. But also because whenever Chichi did you a favor, like lend you money or let you live for free in one of her many apartments, she made you pay it back by treating you like one of her court jesters. Chichi had a posse of court jesters. She referred to them as *mis chicas* (my girls), and they were all lower-middle-class women in their sixties and seventies who owed her favors. Chichi would invite her *chicas* over to her penthouse apartment, which was in La Recoleta, one of Buenos Aires's chicest neighborhoods, just so she could tell them stories of her latest trip to Rome or Paris, and show off the new fashions she'd gotten custom-designed just for her. In Argentina we have a saying: *chupa medias.* It literally means "sock licker" and refers to the act of sucking up to someone. That's what Chichi demanded of her gals. Rita brought me along on all of her sock-licking visits to Chichi's penthouse. For an entire afternoon, I observed my grandma and five other women, who could barely afford their rent, compliment and clap for Chichi as she modeled fur coats and sequined ball gowns for them. At one point, one of the ladies made the mistake of talking about this disease she'd heard about called HIV, which affected men only and caused them to "cry blood" and die, and Chichi scolded her for bringing down the mood.

Chichi had three maids, by the way. One who served her, one who cleaned her house, and one who drove her around.

She'd carry around a tiny bell everywhere she went, which she'd ring-a-ding every time she wanted one of the maids to pour her a glass of wine, light a cigarette for her, or bring her a pastry. Rita may have hated Chichi, but I was fucking obsessed with her and wanted to benefit from her wealth in any way I could. I didn't mind being one of her serfs. In fact, I knew *exactly* how to work that narcissistic queen. One time, Chichi modeled six or seven outfits for us, and it was obvious that the hang was wrapping up. Her *chicas* were fed the fuck up and ready to get the hell out of there. They'd done enough sock licking for a day, but I wanted more! "Chichi, try on that off-the-shoulder gown with the feathers!" I exclaimed. "I want to see it on you again!" You should have seen the death stares the women shot at me for dragging out the session. Rita looked like she wanted to dangle me off the balcony by my feet. But whatever, Chichi loved me and even gifted me one of her silk Hermès scarves that day. Not long after, when my parents ran out of money, we sold the scarf for ten dollars.

My final days in Argentina seemed to take place in fast-forward, as if I had been placed on a people mover and all I could do was observe the things that were happening around me. I was thrown a farewell party at school where I said goodbye to the classmates I was barely starting to get to know. My teacher, who had suspended me for saying that the president was a ball sack, brought a cake for me that had frosting letters reading "Goodbye, Tamaro," which felt like a personal attack. She also gave me a book with two hideous-looking owls on the cover titled *No Place Is Too Far*, which annoyed me for two reasons. One being that the place I was about to move to was really fucking far; it was seven thousand miles far, to be precise. And the second, being that the book had been signed by my garbage Nazi classmates.

Within days, our apartment was completely dismantled. We were moving to the United States with nothing, so we needed to sell every last thing we owned. Every penny counted. At the end of each day, I watched my parents take their small pile of money and count how much they'd accumulated to take with us. Strangers were now entering my apartment and giving my parents cash in exchange for my desk, my Madonna books, and my Kevin Costner poster. "If you buy one picture frame, I'll throw one in for free," I heard Mom say while removing a photo taken of me while performing "All That She Wants" at a state fair. Next thing I knew, there was no furniture left and we'd vacated our apartment so that we could spend our final week in Argentina sleeping on the two twin beds at Nilda's house. The ones we slept on when we arrived. We'd come full circle.

Another reason my final days in Argentina felt like they took place at double speed was that all the trauma of seeing my life dismantled, yet again, led me to spike a fever so high I actually thought I was going to die. My temperature got up to 104 degrees. It was so bad that my pee felt like it was boiling as it was coming out. And, let me tell you, I have *never* barfed so much in my life. I looked like Linda Blair in *The Exorcist*. My skin was green. I was so sick, and so disgusting, that even Hot God abandoned me. He was no longer coming to me during my hallucinations and asking me to count people. Instead, I was all alone in my delirium, floating through dark tunnels that never ended.

My fever was the result of Nilda and Mom having a fight so gruesome and so traumatic for me that writing about it gives me PTSD. Mom had mentioned that she was going to take me to the free state hospital. But Nilda objected, stating that Mom should let her pay for a private children's clinic where I'd get better care. The discussion about what was best for my health quickly escalated into an argument so intense, with *decades'* worth of pent-up reproaches and insults, that in the midst of my delirium, I heard a scream and saw that Mom had sliced Nilda in the forearm with a kitchen knife. At first, I thought I might have been hallucinating from a fever dream, but no, it really happened. For what it's worth, I don't think Mom meant to stab Nilda's arm. It's probably more accurate to say she got carried away while holding a knife. Regardless, there were now *two* of us who required hospitalization.

One week later, after three days in the hospital, I found myself standing in Ezeiza Airport, watching Mom and Nilda embrace and cry as they said goodbye. The stabbing was a thing of the past. If anything, letting out all the shit they'd been holding in had brought them closer together. That day I said goodbye to Pocho and Rita, who had gotten too old and tired to uproot their lives and travel across the hemisphere for us anymore. I said goodbye to Bubaleh, whom I'd never see again. (A few years later, we'd get a call informing us that Bubaleh had passed away in her apartment, surrounded by her cemetery of framed photos of dead relatives. She wouldn't be found until two weeks after her death.) I also said goodbye to Conchita, who handed me a handwritten note. "Open it when you get on the plane," she told me. The letter read:

> *Dear Tamara. Never forget that you are a star. Don't give up what you've started. You know what's in California? Holly-wood. Now go get 'em.*

PART IV

. . . And back to the United States

New–New–New Beginnings
(A Single, Lonely Tooth)

We arrived at LAX in the summer of 1996. Bill Clinton and Monica Lewinsky were at the peak of their affair, which has nothing to do with my immigration story, but I'm throwing it out there because it adds a nice texture. Dad handed over our Argentine passports to a customs and border protection officer. This intimidating chunk-of-a-man with a thick cop mustache held our fate in his hands, as he'd be deciding whether we were trustworthy enough to not overstay our ninety-day tourist visas. I could tell my parents were nervous. Dad kept clearing his throat, something he does when he's uncomfortable or when someone makes him talk about his feelings. Mom, meanwhile, was trying to be sexy and seductive, smiling way too hard and even blowing the officer a fucking kiss as we walked up to his booth.

My main focus was on something else, however: in the immigration checkpoint next to ours, an old woman who looked kind of like a mummy sat in a wheelchair with a blanket draped over her legs, presenting her Mexican passport to a different officer. What specifically got me about this old woman was she had only *a single lonely tooth in her mouth*. I couldn't look away. "That tooth must be so sad and solitary in there," I thought, as I stared into her mouth, barely registering that our designated officer was suspiciously flipping through the pages of our passports.

"What brings you and your family to California?" he asked Dad.

"Disneyland!" answered Dad, putting on the best acting of his life. "I'm going to spend a fortune on these two animals during this vacation," pointing at me and my sister.

"Excited to meet Mickey Mouse?" The officer asked me. I didn't register the question, however, as I was stuck on the old lady's mouth.

"The policeman is talking to you, Tamara!" Mom said murderously, tugging at my shoulder.

"I said, are you excited to meet Mickey Mouse, young lady?" the man repeated.

I looked up at him, with what probably seemed to be the empty stare of a haunted Victorian child, still thinking about that tooth.

"Mickey Mouse has teeth," I said to the officer, who looked so disturbed by my statement that he quickly stamped our passports.

"Hope you stay sane during your vacation, man," he said to Dad with pity. Thus we were officially allowed into the United States of America. The old woman wasn't as fortunate as we were, though. As I walked away, she was being taken into custody by a group of officers.

The four of us pushed our suitcases out of the terminal where we were greeted by a stylish couple in their late thirties: Dina and Freddy Moldavsky. Dina was a high-powered, corporate attorney who wore tailored DKNY suits and had a perfect, redheaded bob. She was elegant, poised, and spoke perfect English with an accent so beautiful it made me want to eat the sound of her voice. Freddy was the exact opposite. He was lazy, rude, and couldn't hold down a job. Sure, he was handsome as hell, and looked identical to George Clooney, but he stayed home all day and only contributed to the household by walking the dog and going to the supermarket.

To remind you, the Moldavskys were an Argentine couple who had been living in California for over a decade and were pretty well off. We'd gotten super close with them during our first time in the United States. When my parents first met Freddy at an Argentine butcher shop in Northridge, they found him to be a repulsive pig. I guess they went up to him and introduced themselves, telling him that they were new in town and could use some Argentine friends. Freddy wasn't in the mood. So he let out a burp, blew it in their direction, and walked away. A few weeks later, my parents bumped into them at Sizzler and confronted Freddy about how rude he'd been to them at the Argentine market. Dina, who clearly called all the shots in that house, was so disgusted by how her husband had acted that she referred to him as a "human dildo," smacked him across the head, and forced him to apologize to my parents, like a child. After that, we became inseparable. The Moldavskys were like family. Our home away from home. In fact, when we returned to Argentina, my parents would talk to them on the phone at least once a week. So when Mom and Dad mentioned how badly we were doing in Buenos Aires, the Moldavskys offered to house us in California until my parents were able to find jobs.

I have to admit that, during the plane ride over, I became kind of fired up about the idea of living in the States again. There were great things about living in California. First of all, according to Mom and Dad, we wouldn't be poor this time around, hopefully. Plus, I'd be closer to Madonna *and* to Payless ShoeSource, my favorite store in the world. But mostly, I was excited because I had a best friend waiting for me in the U.S.: Dina and Freddy's daughter, Bianca. When we were kids, we loved collecting bugs, riding bikes, and touching tongues. We also made our Barbies sit on each other's faces, and do this thing we called "armpitting," where we'd rub one Barbie's vagina against the other's armpit. But that was kid stuff. Now I was twelve and Bianca was eleven, and we would reunite as preteens and do preteen stuff like choreography and talk about boys. As a matter of fact, Bianca and I had spoken on the phone before I left Argentina, and she'd told me she was going to introduce me to all her girl and guy friends, and that we'd all go bowling, or hang out in the Taco Bell parking lot, which was the cool thing to do. During this call, she also mentioned that she showed a picture of me to one of her closest guy friends, a boy named Matt who had green eyes and played water polo, and that he'd looked at it and said I was "pretty fine."

As soon as we exited the terminal, I saw Bianca, with her gorgeous, long, red hair perfectly curled at the ends, and ran up to her with pure, unfiltered joy, but I could instantly tell something had changed. Maybe she was disgusted by the haircut I'd inflicted upon myself before leaving, or maybe it dawned on her that she'd be stuck living with me for a while. Whatever the reason, I was met with a limp embrace and the resentful, sour face of someone smelling cheese. In that moment, I knew I was deeply fucked. The car ride home was a disaster too. I tried making conversation with her as the two of us sat in the back seat of her parent's brand-new Chevy Lumina. "Have you seen *The Mask*?" I asked.

"Yeah," she answered, without even turning to look at me.

"Do you shop at Payless ShoeSource?"

"Ew. No. That's for poor people."

"Yeah . . . that's so true. I hate poor people." And then the two of us sat in silence for the remainder of the car ride.

The Moldavskys lived in Orange County. Ever heard of it? Specifically, they lived in Irvine, a suburb forty-five minutes south of Los Angeles, which was white, upper class, conservative as can be, and was voted eighteen years in a row as the "safest city in America." It was famous for its lack of diversity, its majestic, artificial lakes, its chain restaurants, and its strict police force, known for picking up homeless people the moment they wandered into town and driving them over to Santa Ana, the adjacent city, which was predominantly Latin American. The Moldavskys' house (which would also be mine for the foreseeable future) was like the fucking Taj Mahal to me. It had two stories, a pool with a trampoline, a two-car garage, and a pantry stocked full of flavorful delights: Gushers, Pop-Tarts, Red Vines, and endless Kudos bars. Maybe Bianca wanted nothing to do with me, but I was living in American luxury. Sadly, I quickly learned that these snacks weren't for me to enjoy after I ate a pack of Gushers and overheard Bianca (a spoiled only child who never had to share a thing in her life) crying to her dad that I was eating all her "goodies." To which he replied, "You only have to share with her for a little bit. She's poor. Don't worry, she'll be out of here in no time." This made me feel like a house rat. I contemplated running away, but realized I had nowhere to run away to, because I didn't know anyone else. (This snack incident fucked me up so much that, to the present day, I remain unable to buy myself fun snacks; instead of storing them in my pantry and occasionally indulging, I instead devour them instantly and ferociously, as if someone were about to snatch them away from me.)

That wasn't the only conversation I overheard while living in that house. My second weekend there, Bianca invited four of her girlfriends over. The plan was to get ready at her house and then go to a bowling alley where they'd meet a bunch of their guy friends, including Matt, the water polo boy who thought I was "pretty fine." I stupidly assumed I was invited too, so I got ready for the occasion. I wasn't able to bring many of my clothes from Argentina because we had to make it seem like we were going on vacation, but I put on one of the nicest things I'd brought. This garment was a conversation starter, a statement piece that was an outright hit in Argentina and was bound to make me new friends: an electric blue leather jacket that had a piece of towel (yes, towel) sewn onto the back with a picture of Goofy (yes, Goofy) printed on it. To my surprise, when Bianca's four gorgeous friends arrived smelling like Elizabeth Arden's Sunflowers, with their long, blonde hair pinned back by butterfly clips, and their spaghetti-strap dresses, they looked at me like I was a meatball made of shit. The girls went on to lock themselves in Bianca's room, and I sat in the adjacent room, a room I shared with my parents and my sister, and listened to them laugh about me through the wall, referring to me as "Goofy the F.O.B." "Maybe F.O.B stands for something cool, like Fashionable Older Babe," I thought, not knowing that it actually stood for "Fresh Off the Boat."

I didn't go bowling that night. Instead, I hung out with my parents, my little sister, and Dina and Freddy, who felt terrible about what had gone down. They did what anyone would do to cheer up a preteen: They took me to Cinnabon. As I sat there consuming my large chunk of moist dough, Dina turned to me and said, "I'm sorry about Bianca. She's been acting strange ever since she got that boyfriend."

"What boyfriend?" I asked.

"Matt," Dina answered. "I'm sure you'll meet him soon. He's cute. He plays water polo."

Even though we'd planned to stay with the Moldavskys for a couple of months, we were out after two weeks. We felt like we were imposing, and that's because we *were* imposing. There were simply too many people living under one roof. Dina was kind enough to help us apply for an apartment in a low-income building and got her acquaintances to give us household objects that they no longer needed. Things like a rusty coffee maker, a houseplant that was close to dying but still salvageable, and an old couch that smelled like a wet dog. I treated everything we received like it was made of gold. They were my prized and only possessions. From the *Goosebumps* books that were missing pages to the cardboard box that I delicately draped a piece of fabric on and set next to my bed to use as a nightstand to the industrial crates we stacked to eat dinner on.

The few belongings we had during this time became so precious to me that I focused all my energy and attention on them. So much so that I developed some compulsive habits around them. For example, once a day, I'd take the used Tupperware set someone handed down to us and arrange the containers from the smallest to the largest. I'd then display them on our kitchen counter as if they were my crown jewels. The next day, I'd take them down, mix them up, and do the same thing all over again. Arranging those tuppies from small to large was my favorite thing to do. The Tupperware were my friends.

Another weird-ass thing I started doing was obsessively caressing my mother's back. Everywhere Mom went I followed with my hand slid down the back of her shirt. I scratched and caressed her back while she prepared us delicious bowls of Top Ramen for dinner, while she went to the bathroom to take a piss, or as she pushed a cart up and down the supermarket aisles. I did it so much that I had all her back moles memorized. I even named the moles after some of my old friends in Argentina. There was Betina, the one in the middle of her back, which had a hair coming out of it. Esthercita, Susie, and Eva, the cluster of moles near her lower back that I had to reach down to get to. There was also Maury (named after Maury Povich), the one near her armpit that was more like a skin tag and that I'd constantly pull on, causing her to cry out in pain and slap my hand away.

One time, me and Mom went to get a coffee with Dina's mother, Dorita, who lived in the same apartment building as we did. Dorita was a vile woman in her seventies with a stiff, overly hair-sprayed coif, who would smoke an entire cigarette without ashing it a single time. It was a true skill! She'd suck on her menthol Benson and Hedges, and a long rod of ash would hang off the tip like a limp dick, without ever falling off. Dorita's only topic of conversation was her glory days in Argentina when she was rich. Nothing but nicotine and resentment ran through that woman's veins. That day, as we were sitting on Dorita's couch, which was lined with a see-through plastic cover, I slid my hand down Mom's back and started caressing it. Suddenly, the old bitch stopped mid-sentence, put her coffee cup down, and said, "You're making me uncomfortable with your hand stuck to your mother like that. Get your hand out of there and go play with your friends."

"First of all," I wanted to say, "I don't have any friends," and second of all, "you're not wrong." Instead, I sat there in silence and continued running my fingers over my favorite of mom's moles, Luciano, the one that was shaped like an egg.

Mom and Dad eventually found work driving food trucks, a job they still have today, thirty years later. Every day, they'd leave home at 3:30 A.M., when it was still dark out. They'd stock their trucks with cases of soda and boxes of food, which a cook would prepare in the back, while they drove to various locations around Orange County. When they left for work, my sister and I would stay on our own, which scared the shit out of me. You'd think that being with my sister, having a companion to pass these horrible nights with, would have made me feel less alone. But that wasn't the case. On the contrary, my sister's presence only heightened my terror. I felt responsible her well-being, for calming her down when she woke up crying in the middle of the night, asking where Mom and Dad were. As a matter of fact, I hated my little sister for giving me more things to worry about. I felt rejection toward her because she was a mirror, a constant reminder of the loneliness and the fears I felt at the time.

I barely slept during this period of my life. I was either awoken by Mom and Dad getting ready for work, or by the horrifying sound of a neighbor's cat with an insatiable sexual appetite who decided her favorite place to get fucked was directly outside my window. Regardless of what woke me up, I never went back to sleep. I'd stay awake, going over all the gruesome scenarios that could happen in the middle of the night, for example, a clown breaking into our apartment, raping me and my sister, and cutting us into small pieces, or my parents getting into a deadly car accident and leaving us as orphans. In this scenario my sister and I would get adopted by a ghoulish man with glasses and a combover who would lock us in his basement for the rest of our lives and force us to eat food off the floor like animals, which would, in turn, cause us to develop pig hooves.

At the end of that first summer, I started seventh grade at a godforsaken place by the name of Sierra Vista Middle School, where I didn't know a single soul. The school was composed of hideous concrete buildings and portables that smelled like moldy vaginas. (You may think I'm picking random words to describe the stench in those portables, but if you'd smelled them, you'd know *exactly* what I meant by moldy vaginas.) On my first day of school, my parents asked Dorita if she'd give me a ride. They assured her they wouldn't ask this of her every day, just this once, as it was my first day of school in a new country. The woman didn't work, and she spent all day tanning with the help of those silver reflector things. But she said no because she didn't feel like it. So I memorized the route and walked to school on my own. In Buenos Aires the streets were always filled with people, but Irvine was a fucking ghost town. Unfortunately, no one had ever warned me that in the United States you had to press the pedestrian buttons at crosswalks if you wanted the "walk" sign to turn green. When I reached my first major crosswalk, I waited for the light to change on its own, but it never did. So I stood at that intersection for thirty minutes until a Hispanic woman who was pushing a blonde baby in a stroller walked by and pressed the button for me. You may think it weird that I didn't just cross whenever I saw that no cars were coming. But I stayed in place out of fear that the cops would catch me crossing against a red light and deport me. Because of this, I was over an hour late to school on the first day and was written up. Another very welcoming thing that happened on my first day was that this girl who seemed twenty feet tall told me that if I didn't buy her a Dr Pepper, she'd punch me in the face, and so I did.

My time at Sierra Vista was a depression from hell, and that's putting it lightly. I had no friends. Not one. The only person who spoke to me was Sean, an overweight boy from my math class who sported a bowl cut, wore a T-shirt with Lisa Frank shit on it, and rollerbladed to school. Sean talked about MTV's *The Real World* a lot and was clearly gay, but I thought he had a crush on me, which freaked me out, so I stayed away from him. During lunch, I'd go to the cafeteria, where I was allowed to eat items only from the low-income menu. While the other kids ate cool things like pizza and hamburgers, I was given a bean and cheese burrito and a small carton of milk to wash it down with. Not only would the beans, cheese, and milk combine in my mouth to create a disgustingly thick substance that was nearly impossible to swallow and made me feel like I was going to suffocate, but they also gave me horrible diarrhea, which I'd force myself to hold until I came home from school. After eating, I spent the remainder of lunch walking around the campus in circles, clenching my asshole so I wouldn't shit myself and pretending like I was looking for my "friends"' so that I didn't look like a loser sitting by myself. During these walks I'd always speed walk past Sean who, turns out, was doing the exact same thing.

I was so miserable during this time that I kept a tally of each day that passed, like prisoners do in the movies. My only solace was knowing that, once in a while, I could fake being sick and go home to watch Maury Povich on TV, or to wait for the weekend to arrive so that I could spend all day caressing Mom's back. I have to admit, it took too long for Mom to catch on to the fact that what I was doing was creepy and a cry for help. I think she was taking advantage of having a full-time back caresser, free of charge. I'd certainly take advantage of that if it were offered to me. But eventually enough people pointed out to her that what I was doing was not normal behavior for a thirteen-year-old. Plus, I was starting to get detention a few times a week for how much school I was missing, and I wasn't sleeping, which was causing me to act like a zombie and walk into walls. So Mom and Dad had a talk with me to see what the problem was. "I want to go back to Argentina," I told them. "I hate it here and I don't have any friends."

Mom and Dad had a solution to this problem. They suggested I talk to my homeroom teacher at Sierra Vista. Mom met him on orientation day, and she thought he seemed like a warm and friendly guy. Now, I'm not going to give you this teacher's name so that he doesn't sue me, but if you were to google it, you'd find an article with his mugshot in it, stating that in 2012 he was "accused of kissing a 16-year-old student on the lips while hugging her in the hallway," and of grabbing another girl on the "buttocks." These perturbing incidents hadn't yet occurred when I walked into my teacher's empty classroom, certain he'd have a solution for my loneliness conundrum. "I feel very alone and I have no friends," I said to this six-foot-something grown man who was once a running back in the NFL. The two of us stood there in silence as he thought about a solution. I thought he was coming up with some amazing plan that involved him introducing me to a group of girls who would let me sit with them at lunch or invite me to slumber parties. Instead, he took my hand, caressed the palm of it for just a little too long, and said to me, "You have nothing to fear, Tamara, because . . . *I* am your friend." I left that classroom even more depressed than when I came in, not having achieved a fucking thing and coming to terms with the fact that I was going to have to get used to being on my own. Going forward it was just me, a single, lonely tooth.

The Girl with the Broken Pussy

When Conchita handed me that note at the airport, telling me to not give up what I started, and go conquer Hollywood, I took it seriously. Not just seriously, I took it *literally*. In fact, as soon as my parents were able to buy their first car, a Ford station wagon with exterior wood paneling, four million miles on it, and only one functioning door on the driver's side, which we all had to enter through, I made them drive me straight to Hollywood. In my thirteen-year-old mind, Hollywood (specifically the two or three blocks on Hollywood Boulevard known as the Hollywood Walk of Fame) was where one went to get discovered.

I was able to bring only one of my show costumes when we moved, so I went with my most iconic piece: the black vinyl miniskirt. That's what I wore that scorching ninety-eight-degree summer day, along with my thigh highs and knock-off Dr. Martens. The car ride was so unbearably hot in our A/C-less station wagon that by the time we arrived, my ass cheeks felt like they'd fused with the skirt. As we got out of the car, I filled Mom and Dad in on what the plan would be: We were to start at Grauman's Chinese Theatre and walk east. I'd walk a few steps in front of them, with purpose, like a model on a catwalk, but with a slightly more approachable vibe, all while singing "Vogue," by Madonna, as loudly as I could. A couple of times per block I'd stop singing and perform a spin or strike a pose, then resume walking and singing. It wouldn't take more than a couple of blocks for a talent manager to discover me, stop me, and sign me. That's what I figured managers did all day, after all: stand at corners on Hollywood Boulevard, waiting to discover little girls.

We walked up and down the boulevard for fifteen, thirty, forty-five minutes, but there was no talent manager in sight willing to propel this young star to the next level. After an hour of walking back and forth under the hot sun past an Asian Michael Jackson, two Charlie Chaplins fighting over a street corner, and a Frankenstein missing a leg, Mom's bunion started to throb, Dad had to take a shit, and my ass was completely drenched in sweat, so we were forced to call it. We headed to a nearby McDonald's that smelled like baby diapers and stuffed ourselves with Big Macs and McNuggets.

I'll have you know that I didn't give up that easily. I may have been depressed and friendless, but who the fuck needs friends when you have a dream to be an international pop icon? So a few months later, I gave performing another try. Dad had insisted we become members of B'nai B'rith, a Jewish organization that hosted social events and mixers for Latin American

Jews (Mom hated these gatherings because she claimed that every time she went the same group of cunty women would reintroduce themselves and ask her what her name was, as if they hadn't met her the time before). It was during one of these parties that I asked the DJ if he wouldn't mind playing a CD with a karaoke track of Madonna's "La Isla Bonita" on it, and lending me his microphone. By this point, I'd gotten my period, which caused me to grow a couple of inches and put on some weight. My vinyl skirt was now too tight and made me feel like an encased sausage. My boobs had also started to grow, causing the flesh behind my nipples to expand to lime-sized tumors that were painfully sensitive to the touch. Unfortunately, no one cared to inform me that I should start wearing a training bra, so, during this performance, I wore a white spandex shirt that completely revealed the shape of my tiny little tits. To add insult to injury, halfway through the song, I looked down from the stage at that disinterested crowd of middle-aged people, and my mind went blank, causing me to completely forget the lyrics despite having sung this song a thousand times before. I could tolerate the fact that I was a loser and that I did poorly in school. (I started failing classes after, one day, I happened to look at a popular girl's paper in the middle of a geography test and realized that she was labeling "Brazil" as "Europe" on a map. I figured, if she got bad grades and thrived socially, I should emulate her and stop trying.) But forgetting the lyrics to "La Isla Bonita" was UNFORGIV-ABLE. I was so mad at myself that I brought the microphone up to my mouth and said, "Fuck this shit, motherfucker, you forgot the fucking words," suddenly captivating the attention of the dead-eyed crowd, who was horrified at the curse words I was uttering in front of their young children.

Not long after that nightmare of a performance, a movie came out that shook me to my core. A movie made specifically for me, which combined my two greatest loves: Argentina *and* Madonna. That movie, ladies and gentlemen, was *Evita*. *Evita* awakened a new kind of monster inside me. A monster that continues to inhabit my body and will be with me until my dying day. (In the present, I have actually banned myself from listening to the *Evita* soundtrack, especially when I'm drunk. Hearing it causes me to go into a blind stupor during which I begin to cry, wave my hands in the air, and sing at the top of my lungs, as if possessed by an annoying demon of song, dance, and emotion.) The first time I watched *Evita*, it felt like a sign from daddie god and mommie Madonna to not give up. It was right around that time that my middle school talent show was announced, so I decided to give performing one last chance. I was going to get on that stage and enchant my classmates with a song from the *Evita* soundtrack.

By this time, I had actually made one friend. Her name was Tracy, and she was 80 percent deaf, a ballet dancer, and a fundamentalist Christian. Tracy sat next to me in science class, and I lured her in by telling her that my uncle was Peter Engel, the TV producer best known for creating *Saved by the Bell*. Listen, in my defense, Nilda's maiden name was Engel, so there *was* a small chance that Peter Engel and I were very distant relatives. This wasn't the only time I lied during this period to get people to talk to me. I might have told a few folks, including teachers at school, that I was Evita's niece. They had no way of disproving me, after all. Judge me all you want, but I firmly believe that anyone can be Evita's niece if they want it hard enough. I also spent hours logged on to AOL, chatting with girls my age, pretending to be Kate

Winslet. "Ask me anything about my experience filming *Titanic*," I'd write to some thirteen-year-old in Wyoming. "How was Leonardo DiCaprio?" she'd reply.

"Leo is my best friend," I'd answer. "He's actually *such* a goof and he has B.O. sometimes. But don't tell anyone I said so, hehehe." I didn't limit myself to only impersonating women. After *Meet Joe Black* came out, I pretended to be Brad Pitt for a while. What's absolutely insane about this is that, as an adult, I ended up becoming friends with Brad Pitt, like for real. I spent a summer hanging out with him. "My summer with Brad Pitt," I call it. He once served me the most exquisite charcuterie board I've ever eaten. We played board games, went to concerts, and one time I farted in front of him and the smell was so bad that it made his eyes water, but that's a whole other story. I also pretended to be Posh Spice. There was one girl in particular that I managed to fool for a really long while. Her screen name was AshleyFairy12, and she lived in North Carolina. We talked every day. One time I told her I was having a lesbian affair with Scary Spice. Eventually, Ashley told me that her dad was making her delete her AOL account because he didn't believe that she was chatting with the real Posh Spice and thought I was a child predator. "I know you're the real Posh, though," she wrote. "If you have time, would you mind sending me an autograph," she added, giving me her address. AshleyFairy12 then logged off forever.

Anyways, back to Tracy. Tracy was a bit of a dud. She constantly pressured me to go to her Christian youth groups where some closeted gay dude would tell us that everything was a sin and that we were going to burn in hell and die if we didn't love Jesus. He once devoured an ice cream sandwich in front of us and told us that ice cream was the devil and that now the devil was inside him. I hated it. It made me miss Judaism. But Tracy was all I had, so when I told her I was planning on singing "Don't Cry for Me Argentina" in the talent show, and she answered, "Let me do it with you and instead of singing it, let's do a choreographed ballet to it!" I said, "Of course. I love ballet," even though I didn't.

Tracy and I started our performance by entering the stage in what's known as a ciseaux in ballet, which is a pretty impressive leap where one leg flies in front of the body and the other leg in back, like a wide-open pair of scissors. We wore costumes that Tracy's mom had bought us: white, shimmery dresses with pleated attachments on the back that made us look like we had wings whenever we opened our arms. I'd always been very outspoken and very in control of what I wore onstage, and I initially thought these costumes were totally wrong. They had nothing to do with Evita, a complicated woman who was seen as a whore and a social climber but also a protector of the proletariat. But I was in no position to make demands. I was also a stranger to ballet, a dance that required years of training. So the month leading up to the performance, I practiced my fucking ass off. The practice paid off, because I nailed that initial jump. And I was wrong about the costumes, which turned out to be a hit. During the first minute of the song, I looked out into the audience of pre-teens to get a vibe check and . . . people were into it! This motivated me to keep giving it my all. I spun in place, stood on my toes, and danced like the pro that I was. As I contorted my body, regaining my confidence, I thought to myself, "Maybe this won't make me the most popular girl in school, but it'll definitely put me on the map." We were reaching the end of the song, and Tracy and I began descending into the splits. But as I slid my right leg down the floor, I felt a pop in my groin so loud I was sure that it was audible to the entire auditorium. I then pushed down harder, wanting to finish what I'd started, and felt an intense pain that ran from my vagina down to my thigh and which made my eyes roll to the back of my head. When the music ended, my discomfort was visible to the audience, who gave a slow, scattered applause. I tried to get up and out of the splits, but . . . no go. I was unable to move. The pain was too much. While Tracy got up and took a bow, I sat there holding my crotch, moaning in agony. And then it happened, some teenage twat sitting in the front row yelled out, "She broke her pussy!" Everyone in the audience started laughing. Everyone except for one person, Sean, the gay boy from my math class. He thought it was the most stunning performance he'd ever witnessed.

I was taken off the stage in a wheelchair. My parents were called to pick me up, but they were both at work. The nurse went down the line of emergency contacts until she reached Dorita, Dina's mom. Dorita answered and agreed to pick me up. She happened to be home polishing her gold jewelry with a special cloth she'd bought on the Home Shopping Network. I sat in that wheelchair for an hour waiting to be picked up, which gave me time to think. Mostly I thought about my career and how it was dead. After the shame and embarrassment I'd gone through that day, I told myself I was done performing and promised myself to never get on a stage again. Trying to re-create what I had in Argentina was impossible in the United States. I also realized that the performance *had* put me on the map at school. But unfortunately, not in a good way. Going forward, I'd be known as "the girl who broke her pussy."

My First Love
(A Smear of Feces on a White
Down Comforter)

I mourned the loss of my artistic career in two phases. Phase one included me letting all the anger out on my face. I spent hours upon hours locked in my bathroom, listening to Shakira's *Unplugged* album and Natalie Imbruglia while popping the cystic acne that had sprouted on my chin and cheeks. I squeezed those motherfuckers with the strength of King Kong. Sometimes they'd eject themselves from my face, landing on my mirror in the form of a Jackson Pollock painting. But most of the time, they were too deep to actually pop. Instead, they'd swell into welts that burned with the fury of a volcano and then turn purple. After I got that out of my system, I moved on to step two: channeling my energy into boys.

The first guy who took an interest in me (outside of all the men who salivated while I danced as child) was Eric Grosfeld. I was fourteen when our families met at B'nai B'rith, and I could tell he had a crush on me. Eric was seventeen, and he was uglier than a butthole. He had no lips, rustic brown moles all over his face that resembled ground beef, and he smelled like cum. (I didn't know what cum smelled like back then, of course, but I'd overheard my dad tell my mom that Eric smelled like cum, to which she replied, "The boy is sixteen, he must jack off forty-five times per day. He's probably covered in cum.") A few weeks after I met Eric, I was logged into AOL when an instant message from EGrosfeldHIPHOP popped up. "Hello Tamara. This is Eric. Eric Grosfeld." I was stunned. Before I was able to answer, another message from him appeared on my screen. "I mean this in the most respectful of ways, but I think you're the most beautiful girl I've ever seen." This flattery made me feel a wide array of contradicting emotions. I was terrified at the directness of his comment, slightly revulsed, but also flooded with dopamine from the attention I was getting. Mind you, I had no actual sexual experience at this point and had never even kissed a guy. So I don't know where the hell the next thing I said came from . . .

"I want to sit on your face, Eric," I answered. "I want to take my underwear off, straddle your neck and move my way up. I want to sit on your chin, and then your mouth, and I want to grind my vagina on it." After a few minutes, he replied.

"Wow. Tamara. My beautiful girl. That made me so erect. I think I'm going to put a hole in the wall." I didn't understand what he meant by "hole in the wall," but something told me it meant that he wanted to fuck the wall with his penis because it was hard like a sword. I once walked in on Dad when he was in the bathroom and his penis looked hard like a sword and his testicles looked like two poached eggs. I was so overcome with shame and guilt that I logged off, probably leaving him with a painful pair of blue balls. I was also taken over by an extreme horniness unlike nothing I'd ever felt before. That afternoon, I closed my bedroom door, put a CD single of Celine Dion's "My Heart Will Go On" on repeat and humped the shit out of a life-size stuffed animal shaped like a Saint Bernard, which I'd named Antonio, after Antonio Banderas, until I had my first orgasm.

My affair with Grosfeld had died before it even began. He wrote to me a few more times on AOL but I never replied, and when we returned to B'nai B'rith, I completely ignored him, pretending like nothing had happened. Poor guy. I wonder where he is today. What didn't die was my insatiable desire to masturbate. My god, the number of times I went to town on Antonio Banderas per day was astounding! Eventually, he had to be replaced. He started falling apart from so much humping. Plus, he was too big, which meant I couldn't hide him under the sheets if I wanted to have a quick masturbation at night. I also started getting paranoid that my parents would walk into the room and catch me grinding on it, kissing it, or telling it that I loved it, because the truth is I did love it. I needed a masturbation aid that was smaller and more low-key.

That's when Shlomo the Prayer Bear came into my life. Shlomo the Prayer Bear was a stuffed animal no bigger than my head. He was a bear, but he was also Jewish. He wore a yarmulke and a tallit, and held a little Torah in his paws. I have no idea where Shlomo came from, but, one day, I looked over at the corner of my room and he was lying there, saying "come and fuck me, Tami," and so I did. Oh, how I fucked that devout bear! What a perfect sex toy he was! He fit perfectly in my crotch area and provided the ultimate pleasure without drawing attention to himself. He was also great for travel. I once brought him on a Vegas vacation and quietly masturbated in the king-size bed I was sharing with my mom, dad, and sister. They weren't even sleeping! They were watching *The Silence of the Lambs* on TV, but none of them ever noticed. What a discreet slut my Shlomito was.

I wasn't the only one whose hormones were raging during this Vegas vacation. My sister, who was about eleven, reached puberty early and developed what she referred to as the "dark thoughts." These dark thoughts were a symptom of OCD, which she'd shown signs of throughout her childhood. The dark thoughts involved her having to say certain phrases that popped into her head out loud to us, for fear that if she didn't, the world would come to an end. For example, at any given point of the day, my sister would have to say, "I'm a lesbian. I'm a lesbian. I'm a lesbian." If she failed to say it three times in a row, she was convinced a meteor would come crashing down on the Earth and kill us all. She repeated the lesbian line nonstop during our four-hour car ride to Vegas. She also said it while we rode the gondola under a fake sky at the Venetian hotel, and as we stood in line for the buffet at the New York–New York Hotel.

"It's okay if you're a lesbian," we reassured her. But being a lesbian or not being a lesbian wasn't the point, she *had* to say the words.

To make matters worse, on our way back home we drove past the Luxor Hotel, which was shaped like a giant, black pyramid, when Mom, who was sitting in the passenger seat, turned to me and my sister, and casually mentioned that she'd recently read some prophecy about how the "end of the world would occur when humans built a black pyramid in the middle of the desert." "Here we go," I thought to myself, seeing my sister's expression turn to full-blown terror. Literally nothing worse could have been said to her at that moment. The car ride home was a travesty. The most uncomfortable four hours of my life. My mom's prophecy caused my sister's dark thoughts to worsen exponentially. "I'm a lesbian" felt like a walk in the park compared with what she started blurting out. Now she was saying things like "I want to have sex with a horse," "I want to touch Tamara's boobs," and the most disturbing one of all, "I love Hitler and I think he's a good person." The poor girl must have been in agony. My parents sent her to see a psychiatrist as soon as we arrived home.

Not long after this trip, I started high school. I wanted to start my new school as a blonde, because I'd come to the conclusion that if you weren't blonde, you were ugly and could never be popular, so I attempted to bleach my hair, and burned the shit out of it, leaving it a texture that resembled hay. I also started lining my lips with dark brown liner and then filling them in with clear gloss, which made me look like I was constantly sucking on a pacifier.

I went into high school with very few friends. There was Tracy, of course, who continued dragging me to her church youth groups. Sean, who'd matured over the summer and upgraded his Lisa Frank shirts to a T-shirt that had Cartman's face on it. (Sean, who was still moved and inspired by my Evita performance, convinced me to join Drama Club when we started high school, but my desire to get on a stage had vanished, and I felt safer backstage, helping with lighting or costumes.) I had another friend, Gretchen, who had a horrible case of ADD and would interrupt conversations in order to break out into this annoying Ace Ventura impersonation, her favorite line being "Alrighty then!" And then there was Cassie, who was narcoleptic and would fall asleep whenever I would tell her a story. Believe it or not, Cassie was also a kleptomaniac. She stole money from my wallet when I wasn't looking, then used *my money* to treat me to lunch. Needless to say, with friends like these, guys were staying as far away from me as possible.

But everything changed the moment I met Meg. Meg was a white girl who was born and raised in Orange County, had never left the United States, and was OBSESSED with Latin culture. She had long, blonde hair down to her waist, and big green eyes. Meg was too cool to hang around the popular crowd. She was friends with *everyone*: the drama kids, the punks, the skaters, and the jocks. She was close with the special ed kids and would invite them to Disneyland, using the money her absent father sent her for child support to pay for their tickets. Meg wore bandannas around her hair like Gwen Stefani, navy blue Dickies, and knew how to do the perfect cat eyeliner. I first met her freshman year, in Spanish class. She was trying to learn Spanish because she was dating a Mexican cook who was also a drug dealer, whom she'd met at the restaurant where she worked. He was twice her age, which made him a pedophile, and had a wife and a kid the entire time they dated. I, on the other hand, was taking Spanish class because I was a lazy piece of shit and wanted an easy A.

"Where's your accent from?" Meg asked me on the first day of class.

"I'm from Argentina," I answered, expecting that look of indifference I normally got from people whenever I told them where I was from.

"That's amazing! Aren't there a shit ton of Nazis there? I'm actually dying to go. Not because of the Nazis, obviously. But I heard Buenos Aires is like the Paris of South America." I was blown away. This was the first time since I'd moved back to the United States that someone actually thought it was cool that I was from a different place. I contemplated using my "I'm Evita's niece" line, but she kept talking.

"Did you notice that Mr. Dunn has a huge cock?" she said, then pointed at our Spanish teacher, the whitest, most boring-looking man who ever lived, who wore khaki Dockers that, indeed, showed off the outline of a supernaturally large peen. "How do you say huge cock en español?" she asked.

"Pija enorme," I answered, and watched her scribble it in her notebook.

Mr. Dunn then made us select Spanish names for ourselves, giving us options like José, María, and Lorena. This was problematic for me, and I wanted to tell him to go fuck himself because one can be Latino without having a Latino-sounding name. But I kept my mouth shut because, to be honest, I shouldn't have been taking intro to Spanish in the first place. Instead, I turned to Meg and asked her to pick out a name for me. "Carmen," she said. "You have the energy of a Carmen."

From that day on, she only referred to me as Carmen, and I fucking loved it.

Meg and I became inseparable. Sometimes she'd borrow her boyfriend's cherry red, convertible low-rider, which had a sound system so powerful you could hear it coming from a mile away. We'd pull up to our high school's parking lot blasting Mexican corridos, a type of music popular among criminals and drug dealers, and my god, the white kids in their Volkswagen Jettas and raised F-150's looked at us like we were from a different planet. After school, Meg would come over and eat dinner with my parents so she could practice her Spanish, or we'd go to her house and freely grab beers out of her fridge. The two of us would then sit on lawn chairs in her front yard and make fun of her alcoholic stepdad, a Vietnam War vet by the name of Steve Stevenson, who'd been shot five times (one of those shots was to the head) and spent all day in the garage, playing military marching music at full blast while watching his model trains go around their tracks. "We're such white trash," Meg would say as we watched Steve Stevenson down a twenty-four pack of Natural Light in a single sitting, then start yelling military commands at their dog. "I bet you don't see this kind of shit in Argentina," she'd say to me. She was completely right.

When I turned sixteen, Meg helped me find my first job. She had been forced to quit the Mexican restaurant, after her cook boyfriend went into a jealous rage over her having guy friends at school, causing him to pull over on the side of the freeway and slap her across the face. So the two of us started working as "hat taggers" in the factory of a well-known surfing brand, making minimum wage. It was the easiest job in the world; all we had to do was sit at a table in the middle of a warehouse and put price tags on baseball caps. We were joined by a third hat tagger by the name of Patricia, a fifty-year-old obese woman with a lazy eye who had a lifelong dream of becoming a notary public. Patricia told us she was too fat to walk, so she used an electric wheelchair to get around. She claimed that she had gotten the chair rigged so it would move faster than your average wheelchair. And she was right. The speed with which Patricia would zoom around on it was unreal. It went so fast, she could have probably merged onto a freeway with that thing.

A few days after we started working there, we were sitting at the table tagging hats when Meg turned to her and said, "Hey, Patty girl, you ever had anal sex?" Patricia's eyes lit up. It seemed like she'd been waiting to be asked that question her entire life.

"Have I ever had anal?" she answered, letting out a huge laugh. She went on to describe how it's done in graphic detail. "You want to make sure you're lubed up, ladies," she said, "or it can cause a tear in your rectum and, trust me, you don't want that to happen." For the remainder of our shift, Patricia answered all our sexual inquiries like a pro. It wasn't just the "fun" stuff. Patricia went through every contraceptive method and its efficiency rate, and warned us against the "pull out and pray method," stating that "precum is not something to be toyed with." A true hero that woman was.

The morning after our informative talk, Meg and I showed up to work early, prepared to take in Patricia's knowledge and to set a new world record in hat tagging. We loved our fucking job. But the moment we stepped foot in that warehouse, we were pulled into a conference room where two H.R. representatives told us that someone had overheard us having "inappropriate discussions" at work the previous day and we were being fired for "sexual harassment." Meg and I were kicking each other's legs under that table so hard, we gave each other shin bruises. "Please don't fire Patricia," we begged them before being escorted out by a security guard. "We coerced her into talking about that stuff. It was our fault." We called Patricia at home a few days later to make sure she hadn't been fired.

"I still have my job," she reassured us. "But it's so effing boring there without you. I think I'm going to finally do it. I'm going to quit and become a notary public."

The next job we got was working for a popular chain that sold home goods at a discount price. Within a month of being hired, Meg and I were both promoted to assistant managers and entrusted to close down the store and count out the money in the registers at the end of the night, which is wild because we couldn't have been more than sixteen. I'll have you know that we never stole a single dollar from those registers. Not even a penny. We did, however, fill up entire shopping carts with home goods when no one was around, then transferred all of it to the trunk of Meg's car. It didn't take long for loss prevention to figure out that we were stealing from them. We were both fired six months into working there. Once again, escorted out the door by security guards. Sure, Meg and I might have been wastoids who got fired from two consecutive jobs, but you should have seen our bedrooms! They looked like Versailles, with premium down comforters, sheets of the highest thread count, velour curtains, and crystal-beaded candelabras hanging above our beds.

It was during our junior year that Meg and I decided that teenagers were insufferable and we were done acting like them. We were going to start behaving like rich divorceés in their sixties. We wore fur coats with turbans to school and went to tanning beds multiple times a week, placing a little playboy sticker on our hip before each session so we could see how much color we'd gotten. Tanning was our obsession. It made us feel alive. On weekends we'd go to the beach and lay out for hours, then drive directly to the tanning salon. I fainted from sun exposure on various occasions. My skin had the color, and texture, of a fucking orange.

One day, we skipped school and drove to South Coast Plaza, one of the most upscale malls in California. We used Meg's child support money to buy ourselves matching outfits: black trousers and turtlenecks with rhinestones that spelled out "bebe," and huge black sunglasses that made us look famous. Then we treated ourselves to dirty martinis and veal parmigianas at Maggiano's. It was my first time getting actually drunk, and I did it with style. On the drive home, we smoked cigarettes, which we'd stolen from Meg's mom, and blasted Frank Sinatra. During the ride, which took place in broad daylight, Meg barfed out of her front window while managing to continue driving, and I peed in a supermarket bag in the passenger seat, then chucked the bag out the window into oncoming traffic. Two classy broads.

It was around this time that Bianca, the Moldavskys' daughter, deemed me worthy of being her friend again. I wasn't Goofy the F.O.B. now that I was tan and had Meg, so, halfway through the year, Bianca inserted herself into my life as if nothing had happened. Before Bianca, Meg and I used to have so much fun doing weird things like getting stoned and going to the zoo, taking her pet rats, Bia and Paca, for walks, or driving up to L.A. to see Tom Jones in concert.

But Bianca brought a darkness to our outings. All she wanted to do was hook up with guys, and suddenly, every activity we did revolved around getting attention from men.

After Bianca joined us, the way we dressed started to change. Our shirts got shorter, our bras more padded, and we started wearing our pants low so that our G-strings would pop out the top. Bianca referred to the activities that Meg and I used to do as "pure depression." The only thing that wasn't "pure depression" to her was going to Kokomos, an all-ages nightclub where fifteen-year-old girls could dance with men in their thirties and forties. The three of us would show up to that place dressed like absolute sluts, and men would flock to us like seagulls to a ham sandwich. They'd come up to us on the dance floor and freak dance us from behind to songs like Big Punisher's "Still Not a Player," or Sisqó's "Thong Song," pressing their erections against our young asses until some of them ejaculated. It's fucking disgusting but was somehow legal. I recently found some online reviews that described the place as an "underage meat market" and a "petri dish where pervs thrived." Kokomos has been closed down for many years now, thank god, but I think its owners should be sent to The Hague and sentenced to life in prison for crimes against humanity.

I had my first kiss at Kokomos. I have no idea what the guy's name was, but he smelled like expired Axe Body Spray and looked like a lizard. You know what? It just dawned on me that I was actually fingerbanged for the first time on the Kokomos dance floor as well. It was just me and Bianca that day; our parents had dropped us off after some family dinner at the Macaroni Grill. We were dancing to that song by the Bloodhound Gang about mammals fucking on the Discovery

Channel. Remember that tragedy of a song? Out of nowhere a group of older, buff marines appeared on the dance floor and cornered us aggressively. My first instinct was to get the hell out of there, but then I looked over at Bianca, who was being sandwiched between two of them, and she was on top of the world. I didn't want her to think I was a prude, so I stuck around, when one of them came up from behind me, stuck his hand down my pants and shoved them forcefully into my vagina. I tried to pull away, but he kept me pressed against him. I never even saw the guy's face. The only thing I could tell you about him was that his fingers were thick like sausages.

It took only a few weeks for me to go from my first kiss to my first hand job to my first blow job. Bianca and I would go clubbing and then get into random dudes' cars and suck away. One time I gave a guy a blow job at a park. When I was finished, I realized that there had been a homeless man sitting there watching me the entire time. He was eating a chili dog. Writing this makes me want to die.

The worst part about all of this was that I didn't hook up with guys because I wanted to feel physical pleasure. My body was something for others to enjoy. And to be honest, getting attention from men was oddly familiar. Very familiar, actually. It was similar to what I felt whenever I'd get an older man to make eye contact with me as a preteen. That feeling of power mixed with shame, guilt, and gross horniness.

During all of this, I was still a virgin. Sure, I may have given 780 hand jobs and 400 blow jobs, but I was saving the penetration aspect of it all for someone who loved me. At home, I'd soak in the bathtub for hours and listen to "Kiss Me" by Sixpence None the Richer on my Discman, daydreaming about Nick Carter from the Backstreet Boys. In my fantasy we'd be lying on the beach, dressed in white flowy linens, watching the sun set. First, we'd exchange a passionate tongue kiss, and then he'd stare into my eyes and say, "Would you like to lose your virginity to me, Tamara?"

"Yes, Nick. I would," I'd answer. He'd then push his fat (but kind of short) penis inside me, and we'd both cry of how much we loved each other. I couldn't tell you why Nick Carter had a short and fat chode in my fantasy. He just did.

In real life, my first love story went a little differently.

I met Jason while standing in line for the bathroom at a depressing house party that Bianca had begged us to go to because she was trying to hook up with some bro-ey dirtbag that was on Accutane and had lips so flaky they looked like spanakopita. When it was my turn to go into the bathroom, Jason forced his way in behind me. This should have been a red flag, but he was so cute, wearing Acqua Di Giò, and a black hooded Etnies sweatshirt, the brand that all the hot guys wore at the time. "I just want to talk to you," he said, turning around to face the wall while I peed (what a gentleman). At seventeen, Jason had just gotten out of rehab for the third time. Not only was he an alcoholic, he'd recently overdosed on painkillers, which he'd stolen from his mom. Jason had been adopted as a young boy by a very wealthy family that threw money at him but completely neglected him. He was a fucking disaster. But there was a lovable sadness about him that got to me and made me want to take care of him.

I started going over to his parents' beach house almost every day. There were never any parental figures around, so we'd make out all over the house. "You have beautiful lips," he told me after our first kiss, "you just have to learn how to use them." Weirdly enough, Jason was never pushy with me. This wasn't because he was a gentleman, but because he was fucked up all the time and couldn't get it up. Most of the time we'd dry hump and he'd go down on me. Then, one night, he showed up to my parents' house in the middle of the night, wasted out of his mind, and started throwing pebbles at my window. I ignored the fact that he was blacked out and focused on the idea that someone was throwing pebbles at my window, which made me feel like this was *Romeo and Juliet.* I let him in and begged him not to make noise so as to not wake my parents. In my room, he managed to get a boner for about thirty seconds during which I lost my virginity. After that sad attempt, Jason stumbled down the stairs, bumping into furniture, saying unintelligible words. He then walked into my kitchen, opened my refrigerator, pulled down his pants, and pissed inside it. After he left, I spent an hour on my hands and knees, cleaning his piss from my fridge so my parents wouldn't notice. My beautiful first love.

And then, when I was close to finishing senior year, Meg told Bianca and me that her mom and stepdad would be going on a Margaritaville cruise for a few days, so we threw a big graduation party. I felt so incredibly cool that night. Not only because I wore a fake, magnetic lip ring, and because I'd procured some ecstasy from a guy in my science class who was obsessed with Gwar, but because I was going to introduce Jason to all my friends. An hour into the party, Meg and I took our ecstasy pills. It was our very first time. While we waited for them to kick in, Meg put on a banana costume that she had lying around and led a few of us on an expedition in search of treasures in her crazy stepdad's room. What we found in that man's drawers truly rattled us to our very cores.

There were a variety of guns, half-eaten baked bean cans, a hand grenade, a human molar, and a stack of vintage VHS porn that was *all* alien-themed. The way we screamed as we went through those titles, among which were *Spermula, Sex Trek: The Next Penetration, The Perils of Gwendoline in the Land of the Yik-Yak,* and the pièce de résistance, which we played on her big-screen TV for the entire party: *E.T. Porn Home.* As a big group of us watched a female E.T. with huge titties say things like "I miss my home planet" and "I have so much to learn from humans" while getting plowed from behind, I noticed that Bianca and Jason had been missing for a while. I instantly had a bad feeling about this.

"Meg, you have to see this! There are actual smears of feces all over your down comforter," screamed Sean (earlier that year, Sean had gotten mono and lost a fuck ton of weight, officially came out as gay, got his tongue pierced, and moved on from Cartman shirts to metallic silver shirts). Meg and I ran into her bedroom thinking this was a joke. It was not. The entire room smelled like poo poo, and there were actual smears of feces all over her white down comforter, which Meg violently pulled from her bed and dragged to the living room, where about thirty teenagers, including Bianca, were partying. "Who the fuck took a shit on my bed?" Meg yelled. The room went silent, except for Enrique Iglesias's "Bailamos," which continued blasting on the sound system. Some people laughed. Others, including Bianca, acted outraged that someone would do such a thing and came up to examine the evidence on the comforter, trying to convince us that it was "just chocolate." Jason was nowhere to be seen. While Meg and I continued questioning people to see if anyone had seen or heard anything, we were approached by Andy, Jason's best friend, whom he'd brought to the party. "Listen," Andy said, looking at me specifically. "I'm only telling you this 'cause you seem like a nice person, but Jason and I just tag-teamed Bianca in that room. That girl is a sex freak. Jason and her ended up having anal and she shit everywhere. It was too much for me, so I bailed. But hey, you should break up with Jason, the two of them have been fucking for weeks." I felt like a horse had kicked me in the chest and I was about to die. All I could do to stop myself from crying was focus on one of the shit smears on Meg's comforter. As Andy kept talking, I felt a tingling sensation take over my body and noticed that the shit smear was starting to change shape and move with the beat of the music. That's when I realized the ecstasy was kicking in.

That Crazed Look of Psychosis

I'm going to get into what came to be of Bianca and Jason in a bit. But first I want to rewind to when we first moved to Irvine and talk about my mother. My mommie dearest. Back then, as I was about to start middle school in a new country, I was literally attached to Mom. Remember my desperation with scratching and caressing her back all day? I've always interpreted the caressing of her back as an act of self-soothing. As long as I had my hand slid down her shirt and I was touching her, I felt calm. I was connected to my mother, and it meant I wasn't alone. My interpretation was completely erroneous, however. Now that I'm older and I can reflect on it, I realize I wasn't caressing her back to soothe myself. I was doing it to soothe *her*. I was doing it because I wanted *her* to feel calm and at ease. I was caressing my mother the way a parent caresses an infant.

Now the question at hand is, why in the lord's ass was I in such need to appease my mother? Well, there's a few layers to it. One reason was that Mom is a depressive person who also suffers from borderline personality disorder. She can go from catatonic to volcanic in seconds, and you never know what will spark it. Immigrating back and forth all those times and having to start from scratch didn't help. But this time around was particularly bad. (The first time we moved to the States, she was younger. She had more energy, more hope. Plus, in the eighties there was slightly less of a crackdown when it came to immigration. For example, if you were a tourist, you could obtain a driver's license, which made your life generally easier.)

This time around, however, the heaviness of being undocumented immigrants weighed on us more, especially on Mom, whose mental state was already fragile. There was the time when someone left an empty bag of McDonald's near my parents' car, and our racist neighbor blamed Mom and Dad for it, spray-painting the side of their car with the words IN THE U.S.A. WE THROW OUR TRASH IN THE GARBAGE. There was the fact that we couldn't leave the country (if we wanted to come back, that is). We didn't have social security numbers, which meant my parents couldn't legally work (I wouldn't be able to either when I came of age). They were also unable to obtain driver's licenses, which meant that getting pulled over for something basic like not signaling could potentially lead to a deportation for the entire family. Our only hope was to, one day, win the green card lottery. The green card lottery, also known as the Diversity Immigrant Visa Program, grants about fifty thousand permanent resident cards per year to a number of countries around the world. Dad applied for us every year, but it was a long shot, as more than twenty million people apply annually.

All that to say, Mom wasn't at her best. And there I was providing physical comfort for her. The other big reason I was compelled to do this was that I felt like I'd failed her. In Argentina, when I was at the peak of my child performing days, I was the perfect daughter in my mother's eyes (having her see me as the perfect child was a problem, in and of itself, because I got used to her adoration, and the moment it was gone, I was left having no fucking clue where my self-worth was supposed to come from). As you know, in her youth, Mom was also a dancer, so during my days as a performer she saw herself in me. It would be a stretch to say she got to live out what she didn't accomplish through me. But in my glory days I was an extension of her that she was proud of.

Unfortunately, after we moved back to the States, I attempted to get back into performing and failed. The shame and embarrassment of walking around Hollywood Boulevard looking for a manager, forgetting the lyrics to "La Isla Bonita" at B'nai B'rith, and breaking my pussy in front of my entire middle school led to the decision that I was never going to get on a stage again. The moment I stopped performing, I was no longer a perfect child for Mom, and all that she was left with was a depressed, introverted, acne-ridden teenager. I was now an extension of her but, like, in a bad way. Like an unsightly wart. Not only could she not cope with the fact that her star had turned into a loser, but she thought I was doing it on purpose, to spite her.

"Why don't you invite a couple friends over?" Mom asked me during my first year of middle school after she found me alone on a Friday night, lying on the couch, cupping a fart and then smelling my hand. (I know, I was not at my best, but we had literally *just* moved here and smelling my own farts brought me comfort.) "In Argentina you had so many friends," she added, twisting the knife. A few weeks later, I tried to show Mom that I *did* have friends, so I invited Tracy over to watch *Spice World*. At some point in the evening, Mom came up to Tracy with a tray full of burned sausages that Dad had just grilled out on the balcony. "You want a chorizos, honey? They looks like penises, but taste delicious," Mom said to the whitest, most religious girl in the universe, who started crying and called her parents asking to be picked up. Mom, unable to understand why my new friend reacted so poorly to her joke, came into my room that night with complaints. "That girl is dead alive, Tamara. What a boring human being! If she ever comes back here, I'm going to shock her with a defibrillator and bring her back to life."

In eighth grade I invited Sean over, thinking she'd find him more fun than Tracy. That didn't seem to satisfy her either. "Your leitmotif is hanging out with gays," she said to me after he'd left. "How are you ever going to meet a guy if all you do is gay, gay, gay?" (Today, Mom begs me to bring my gay friends over.) Finally, in high school, I started dressing slutty and going to the all-ages club hoping I'd meet a guy, just like she wanted. At this point, Mom's issue was no longer "how are you going to meet a guy?" but "what kind of guy are you going to meet at these clubs?" And, every time, she'd end the critiques with the reproach that I was doing this TO her.

During my high school years, dinnertime was always the worst. Sometimes we'd be sitting at the table, and Mom would ask a question like "what did you do today, Tamara?" I quickly came to learn that those simple questions were always posed with the goal of critiquing some aspect of my life. It didn't matter what my answer was. I could have said, "Mother, today I made a plane fly into the Twin Towers and caused 9/11," or "Mother, today I single-handedly cured the cancer of every orphan in the world," and Mom would find a way to turn it against me. These dinnertime talks, during which she'd always remind me that I had no self-esteem (fine, it was true, but how was her reminding me helping?), were becoming more and more frequent, and I could usually predict if a bad one was coming based on how depressed or volatile she was that day. I have always, ALWAYS, been extremely aware of my mother's moods. For the first few years, I'd apologize for the things that bothered her about me, about who I inherently was as a person, and try to find ways to please her and appease her. But as I got a little older and more rebellious, I was no longer willing to caress my mother's back every second of the day, and I got so sick of her critiques that I started to fight back. "You're being a bitch, Mom," or "You're acting crazy," I'd yell across the dinner table when she started attacking me. But whenever I fought back, she'd lose her mind. Me calling her "crazy" was a huge trigger for her. She'd get this crazed look of psychosis in her eyes, and it was like a demon took over. She'd become explosive, grabbing me by the arms and shaking me around, then threatening to kill herself because of "how awful I was to her." Whenever things escalated to this point, I'd start hyperventilating and go into this horrible state of panic where I felt utterly insane because I couldn't figure out what the fuck we were even fighting about, or what exactly I had done to upset my mother *this* badly.

It was around this time of peak fighting that my aunt Sandra came to see us in the United States. Sandra had ended up marrying Mateo, the cute Mexican guy she met while salsa dancing during our first time living in the United States. When we returned to Argentina, she actually stayed with him in the United States, and a few years later, the two of them had moved to Mexico City after he'd gotten a big job teaching philosophy or some shit. While living in Mexico, Sandra became isolated and stopped receiving treatment for her schizophrenia and other mental disorders. She had lost an abnormal amount of weight, and all her teeth started to fall out, which led her to get dentures. These dentures didn't fit her properly, however, so they were constantly shifting inside her mouth. During her visit to us, Sandra suffered a pretty severe schizophrenic episode. The only thing she wanted to talk about was how she'd become pen pals with Bill Clinton. "Bill and I are the best of friends," she said to us during dinner one night. She said it so manically that her dentures slipped out of her mouth and she caught them with her hand before they hit the table. She popped her teeth back in and kept talking, "I offered to give Bill Spanish lessons and he took me up on it. We're going to start meeting at Starbucks once a week." Mom was so upset that, at least for this one dinner, I was spared her nightly critiques.

The Bill Clinton comments were nothing compared with what happened next. When we woke up one morning, we realized that Sandra had gone missing. We drove around town for hours looking for her, and just as we were about to call the police, we got a phone call from a nice man, stating that he'd found Sandra walking on the side of the 5 freeway. When we picked her up a few towns over (she'd walked twelve miles), we found Sandra dressed head-to-toe in clothing with the American flag printed on it. "Where were you trying to go, Sandra?" my mom asked, terrified.

"I'm trying to get to Washington, D.C., so I can become an American citizen," Sandra answered. That's when I noticed it. My aunt was looking at us with that same crazed look of psychosis that Mom had, but way, way more intense. At that moment, I also realized where Mom's fear and sensitivity to being called "crazy" stemmed from.

Mom didn't let Sandra return to Mexico. It turns out that Mateo had become an alcoholic and was emotionally and physically abusive to her. So Mom arranged for Sandra to move back to Argentina to live with Pocho and Rita. Pocho had suffered a heart attack a few years before this and was forced to retire early, at which point Mom had to start sending money to cover her parents' expenses and health insurance. Even though Mom was barely starting to establish her own life in the United States, and still dealing with the pressures of being undocumented, she now had the added responsibility of having to financially support her parents and her sister.

This brings us back to the comforter shit-smear fiasco, which happened shortly after Sandra visited us, and when I was months away from graduating high school. The fallout went as follows: After much interrogation, Bianca finally admitted to having had a threesome with Jason and Andy on Meg's bed. At first, she vehemently denied that she'd shit on the comforter (and tried to blame it on Meg's dog), but she eventually came clean about that too, and gave Meg ten dollars to pay for the dry cleaning. She then called me five times a day for the next couple of days asking me to forgive her. At first I ignored her calls, which gave me a minor sense of control over her for once, but eventually I agreed to meet her at P. F. Chang's so that we could sit down like two adults and hash things out over chicken lettuce wraps. "How could you do that to me?" I asked her. "I swear to god, I didn't realize what I did was *that* bad. I'm straight-up dumb!" she said. "You should have told me you didn't want me to fuck him," she added. (By the way, I have to add that, later in life, I ended up finding out that Jason and Bianca actually dated for two years after this, behind my back.)

I never saw Jason again. But I did end up forgiving Bianca. Partly because I was a pushover who was scared of being alone and had no self-worth. But also because of my parents. Their attitude about what happened between Bianca and Jason was along the lines of "it's just stuff teenagers do" and "the Moldavskys did so much for us." These dismissive reactions from my parents weren't what hurt me most; it was the comments insinuating that maybe Jason fucked Bianca because of something *I* had done wrong. For example, how Bianca was so "put together" and always looked "impeccable." Not only was it upsetting to hear the people who were supposed to defend me refer to the person who hurt me as "impeccable," it also signified that I was *not* impeccable.

It wasn't long after this that some good news came our way when we got a phone call from our immigration lawyer, a Chabad-Lubavitch Jew with the most volatile temper I've ever witnessed, informing us that we'd won the green card lottery. The call actually came when we were sitting at dinner. I'd just informed Mom that I wanted to move to San Juan, Puerto Rico, so that I could live with a gorgeous Puerto Rican bass player I'd met at a reggae concert the week prior (hahahahahahahahahahaha). By this point I was pushing her buttons on purpose.

"Congratulations," our lawyer told us. "All you need to do is show up at your appointment where you'll receive your permanent residence cards. It'll be quick and they won't ask you any questions," he reassured us. A week later, the four of us sat in a tiny office inside the Immigration and Naturalization building in downtown Los Angeles, ready to accept our legality as humans.

Our interview sure was quick. In fact, it lasted all of thirty seconds. That's because the immigration agent opened up our passports, noticed that we had overstayed our expired visas by a number of years, and deported us on the spot. He didn't give a single shit that we'd won the green card lottery. We'd broken the law, so we were out. Dad, my sister, and I had to physically carry Mom out of that building. Dad then called our lawyer, who showed up thirty minutes later with mustard and ketchup stains all over his shirt, ready to put up the fight of his lifetime. "This is absolute fucking horseshit," he screamed while pounding at the door of the immigration office. The man was possessed by some sort of Jewish devil. His skin had gone from white to beet-red, and he was yelling at the top of his lungs in a high-pitched voice that could pierce through the thickest of ear drums. "This family has been deported on wrongful terms and I will call every news outlet and get them down to this fucking building if you don't let me in and correct this, motherfuckers." Ten minutes later, and after a half-ass apology from some mid-level bureaucratic rat at the immigration office, we were undeported and our green cards were accepted.

In the spirit of self-soothing, my family and I drove straight from the immigration building to our forever happy place: the mall. We walked around in a daze. I bought a silver tube top at Wet Seal. We then headed to the food court and ordered some slices of pizza from Sbarro. After we finished eating, my sister said she didn't feel good and instantly barfed all over herself. Dad kept saying the pizza had made her sick, but it was probably just the tension from the incredibly shitty day we experienced. Regardless, he took her to the bathroom to get cleaned up. Mom and I were left on our own. Mom looked like she'd had the life sucked out of her via a suction hose. "Aren't you even a little bit happy?" I asked her, trying to get her to focus on the fact that we'd just been granted our residency.

"How can I be happy after the day I just lived?" She scoffed. "How can I be happy when I've had to start from zero over and over again? Why do bad things only happen to me?" she added. Feeling sorry for herself, she began sobbing in the middle of the food court. I suddenly felt nothing but pure hatred toward her. I'd lived through the exact same shitty experience as her that day. We all had! In fact, I paid attention to *my* body for once, and I felt like I'd been beat up with a baseball bat. Yet there I was trying to cheer *her* up, trying to make *her* happy. I felt like I was going to lose it. My level of contempt toward her was unlike anything I'd ever experienced before. I was enjoying watching her cry. It felt wrong to have such feelings toward my own mother.

"WHAT ABOUT ME!?" I screamed back at her. I was so loud that everyone sitting nearby at the food court turned to look at us. "What about how I feel? Does *that* matter?" I added, slamming my fists down on the table, completely taken over by that same crazed look of psychosis that I'd seen on her and my aunt Sandra. "You always think bad things only happen to you!? I've lived through the exact same experiences as you." I was overflowing, yelling at the top of my lungs. "But you had the choice to move from here to there and start from zero! I DIDN'T!!!" I knew I'd gotten through to her. I could see it in her face. We sat in silence for a few seconds.

"I'm sorry, daughter," she answered, covering her face with her hands.

"It's okay," I replied. My rage had subsided, and the two of us were now softly crying.

"I love you, Tamara."

"I love you too, Mom." I answered. I was overcome with guilt because of how bad I'd exploded on her, so I walked up to her and we held each other for a moment.

"We've both suffered, equally," she added. (Of course she had to get that last "equally" bit in.)

"Yes, Mom, we've both suffered, equally," I answered. I then slid my hand down the back of her shirt and began caressing her back, becoming reacquainted with all her moles.

The Interpreter

Not long after I graduated from high school, Nilda immigrated to the United States and came to live with us. This happened after a summer when she went kind of crazy and, as a result, burned every single one of her family photos. She blamed this outburst on the hot weather, stating that the Buenos Aires heat made her feel insane. First, she tried moving to the Yiddishland countryside, which didn't quite work out for her. She claimed to have gotten shunned from the Yiddishland social circles and Rummikub groups because she was fat. This was partly true. But she was mostly shut out because she tried getting revenge on some of the women who were commenting on her weight by spreading rumors that their husbands were homosexuals and liked to "take it in the ass." This drama died down, but then Nilda nearly burned down all of Yiddishland when her stove caught fire while she was cooking her signature meatloaf with a whole egg in the center.

(Only some of us on this blessed Earth had the pleasure of savoring her signature meatloaf with a whole egg in the center.) That she'd almost burned down Yiddishland did not particularly bother her. But the embarrassment of people knowing she'd burned her food like a goddamn amateur made her want to leave not only Yiddishland but the country altogether and move to the United States.

Just before she arrived, Mom and Dad found themselves making a decent amount of money for the first time in their lives. This change of luck happened because of a suicide. I'll explain. One of Mom and Dad's acquaintances, who worked at Disneyland and was always giving us free tickets to the park, shot herself in the head after her husband left her for a woman half her age. The news was upsetting for two reasons: First, she was a really nice person who didn't deserve to die, and second, our Disneyland hookup was now deceased, and we'd have to start paying for our own tickets. During this woman's service (for which she left a suicide note stating that her dying wishes were that she be buried in her wedding dress, that her cheating husband be forced to attend *and* give a speech, and that all her guests had to get as drunk as possible), Mom drank one too many margaritas and got flirty with one of the dead woman's co-workers, some man who was a higher-up at the Anaheim Disneyland park who told Mom she had a "banging body." When Mom mentioned that she and Dad operated a food truck, this kind and generous man, who totally wanted to fuck my mom, instantly offered her access to the park's backstage so that she could provide food services for all Disneyland workers. Mom and Dad were used to providing food for small construction sites here and there, so catering to the entire Disneyland staff was a big fucking deal. Seeing dollar signs in this man's eyes, Mom opened up the first button of her shirt, revealing her cleavage a tiny bit more, planted a kiss on the man's cheek, and said, "Absolutely, honey. I DO IT."

A few months later, the bottom of my parents' mattress was overflowing with hard-earned casharooly from selling tacos, chow mein, and hamburgers (the menu options of their truck really took you on a culinary journey) to Disneyland employees. They served the mechanics, the ride operators, and the iconic characters that we all know and love like Minnie Mouse (a man in his sixties who came up to the truck every day smoking a cigarette, wearing only the bottom half of the costume) and Snow White (who was always ordering fried food to cure her hangover and often complained about being on her period). This opportunity allowed my parents to finally achieve the American dream they'd always longed for and buy a two-story house with a swimming pool just before Nilda arrived.

The Southern California weather was perfect for my grandma. From the moment she moved in with us, she chilled out and spent the majority of her days dressed in her gold, one-piece bathing suit, floating face-up in our pool. The woman was thriving. Sometimes she invited over Dorita, Dina's mom, and the two of them would float together and argue for hours. They never ran out of subjects they disagreed on, from whose diabetes was more severe to who had gotten the most charred from the sun to who made the best potato salad.

I loved having her at home. Not just because we had a full-time chef living with us, but because now I had family living in the U.S. Nilda was also cool as fuck. She was in her floating phase, and down for whatever. One time I asked her to give me a mullet, and she did so, with a pair of kitchen scissors. Another time, she drove our cleaning lady to get an abortion after she'd been impregnated by our neighbor's gardener. Nilda was in such a rush to get to the abortion on time that she forgot to open the garage door and drove straight through it, completely destroying not only the garage but Dad's car. (Our cleaning lady saw the crash as a sign from God to keep the child and ended up naming the baby Nilda.)

As for me, I had been freed from the painful inferno that was my high school years and was entering a very interesting and fun time in my life: my groupie phase. It all started earlier that year when Meg and I attended a Latin rock festival at the Universal Amphitheatre. We were sitting in the audience when a pig-faced man approached us and asked us if we wanted to go backstage. He hung all-access laminates around our necks, escorted us back, and next thing you know, we were taking mushrooms and doing human pyramids with one of Mexico's most famous rock bands. That night, we exchanged emails with dozens of musicians. We had just turned eighteen.

From then on, every time a Latin band came to town, Meg and I would drive up to L.A. to hang out with them. Sometimes we'd sell them weed. One time, a band from Venezuela called us looking for cocaine, and we sold them crushed-up Midol. A few times we gave them hand jobs if they were cute or really liked their music, but the majority of the time we were doing weird shit like mummy-wrapping ourselves with toilet paper or lining the hotel room floors with squares of Kraft cheese singles.

It wasn't just Latin American artists. One time we were so stoned that we got on a tour bus with a really well-known rapper, not knowing where it was headed and were forced to get off when we realized we were about to cross the border into Tijuana without our passports. We got invited to the

Oscar party for the Mexican film *Y Tu Mamá También*. David Schwimmer was there for some reason, and Meg went up to him and said, "What the fuck are *you* doing here? You're white."

"You're white too, you asshole," he replied, and then they both started laughing.

On my nineteenth birthday, we hung out with Stevie Wonder, and at some point during the night, we got into a limo with some record label execs and struck up a conversation with a well-known music agent. "Do you two have any interest in being in the music business?" she asked us. The next month she got us both internships with record labels. I fit in so well with the team that I got hired a few months into the internship. I was driving to Beverly Hills every day, putting together press releases and buttering up radio hosts so that they'd play our artists' records. These were the good old days in the music industry, too, before the streaming era, when labels were burning through money like there was no tomorrow. One time the head of the label was too lazy to accompany one of our biggest artists, a hunky, Mexican ranchera singer (who was also a famous telenovela actor) to an awards show and asked me to go in his place as a representative for the label. I was given a company card and sent to Neiman Marcus, where I bought myself an expensive sequined suit and got my hair and makeup done. Then, I walked the red carpet alongside this muscular stud who wore a big hat and charro-style suit. "Whatever you do, don't fuck him," the head of the label told me as he sent me off to the awards, adding, "I hear he's horrible in bed." At the end of the night, the singer invited me over to his hotel room for champagne, and I disregarded my boss's advice and fucked him anyway. The sex was just as bad as I'd been warned. He did have a gorgeous hairy chest and remarkably small balls, though.

My parents, especially my mom, seemed to love that I was working in the music industry. So I was genuinely taken by surprise when, a few years into my job, they sat me down one evening for a serious talk about my future. "We think you should stop wasting your time following those artists around and become a Spanish interpreter." I blinked at them, uncomprehending. "We heard you can make a fortune as an interpreter. You'll be able to buy a house," they added. The reason for my parents' sudden desire for me to shift careers turned out to be that the previous night, they'd gone out to dinner at Buca di Beppo with the Moldavskys. The entire evening, Dina and Freddy boasted about this new friend of theirs who was making a killing working as an interpreter for doctors and lawyers. "Tamara should do it. She's got a great mastery of both languages and is wasting her time following those artists around. She'd be able to buy a house." I shut this horrible idea down the moment my parents suggested it. I loved my job and could see a path to becoming an executive at the record label. I was even starting to work closely with the A&R department, going to shows and helping them discover new bands. But the Moldavskys' opinions were so sacrosanct to my parents that they continued pushing the idea of me becoming an interpreter every time they got the chance. Until, one day, I started believing that this was a great idea and convinced myself that I really wanted to buy a house. (I was still living with my parents in my early twenties, which is normal for Argentines. In fact, living with your parents until you're in your thirties isn't totally uncommon in Argentina. I have a cousin who lived with his parents till he was thirty-four. His mom washed his dirty underwear by hand and made his bed for him every day.) But the idea of buying this house and becoming an interpreter was hammered into my brain so much that I quit my job at the label and started practicing for the interpreter's certification exam.

The exam had two parts: a written portion where you were asked to translate medical and legal terms like appendectomy and misdemeanor, and an oral portion in which you had to wear headphones and interpret an audio recording from Spanish into English and vice versa, using both consecutive and simultaneous methods. The specific recording I'd gotten was a reenactment of an exchange that took place in a hospital between a doctor and a Spanish-speaking mother whose newborn was vomiting blood. I should have taken those headphones off then and run as far away as possible. Instead, I committed to the bit, not missing a single word that the mother said, even matching the desperation and shakiness in her voice, and passed the exam on the first try.

I quickly learned that there wasn't as much money in interpreting as I'd been promised. Sure, I'd get paid sixty dollars to interpret a thirty-minute doctor's appointment for a man who'd gotten his big toe run over by a forklift, but I'd have to drive two hours to get to the hospital I'd been assigned to, and two hours back. Moreover, interpreting jobs weren't as easy to come by as I'd been told, and sometimes I'd get only a few jobs a week, so I was basically earning minimum wage. Eventually I realized that the only way to make a living with this profession was to establish relationships with specific doctors who saw a number of Spanish-speaking patients per day and would allow me to become their in-house interpreter. I worked for so many goddamn doctors. There was a psychiatrist who drank wine coolers from a coffee cup while treating her patients. A urologist who specialized in erectile dysfunction, where I'd find myself interpreting phrases like "Doctor, is it normal for my penis to look this weird?" or "Doctor, my problem is that I can only ejaculate if I'm thinking about having sex with my sister-in-law." I also worked for doctors who were sexual predators, who gave me jobs as long as I didn't say anything if they grazed my ass with their hand in passing. For a while, I even worked for a women's prison where I got to witness a case of mouth herpes so severe the inmate's tongue had swollen to the size of a melon. Regardless of how much I worked, though, I was far from making enough money to buy that house. In fact, I wasn't even able to afford to move out of my parents' house.

Another issue with this job: It made me psychotically miserable. My days, which during the previous year had been filled with lunches and music events, were now spent in fluorescent-lit waiting rooms and exam rooms, filling out medical questionnaires and interpreting for racist doctors who'd often verbally abuse their Spanish-speaking patients and treat them like dog shit. The worst part was that I was completely powerless because, in this job, I wasn't supposed to exist. I wasn't paid to have thoughts or opinions on how these people were treated; I was there to stand against a wall and repeat what everyone around me said. In fact, one day, while standing in a gastroenterologist's office, staring at a poster that read "Do you suffer from leaky gut syndrome?" while listening to a patient complain about having a fistula (look it up, or actually, don't), I was suddenly hit with the realization that I was the furthest away I'd ever been from the performer I once was. And the worst part was, I had zero energy or desire to even attempt to get back to it. I was too far gone.

I was about twenty-five when I started experiencing a very classic case of depression: a lack of motivation, and a general air of negativity and doom. I don't know why it hit me when it did. Maybe it was that I got older and the weight of my destabilizing childhood started getting to me. Maybe I was mad at myself for getting talked into quitting the record label. But this depression was a long time coming. To make matters worse, Meg moved to Cancun around this time because she fell in love with some cokehead she met on MySpace who sold timeshares for a living. Her departure killed me. I became totally isolated and started throwing around the phrase "I want to die" so much that I eventually saw a psychiatrist who put me on twenty milligrams of Prozac, which helped me feel normal again. I also started smoking weed and became a full-blown stoner. I'd get up in the morning and wake and bake on the toilet while taking my morning shit. Then I'd drive to work and, before entering, take a hit off my very discreet pipe that was shaped like a penis with veins. After that, I'd smoke once an hour until I fell asleep at night. I had this huge stash of schwag that Meg had gifted me before she left, which I kept in a gift box from Gap. I also smoked a fuck ton of cigarettes. My car was covered in empty packs of Parliament Lights, and water bottles full to the brim with cigarette butts. One time I counted, and there were twenty-seven empty packs of cigs in my car. Sometimes, I'd show up to work wearing my pajamas under my clothes or wearing two different shoes. I was straight-up nasty. I had skid marks in my underwear and smelled like Charles Bukowski. But who cared? No one noticed me anyway. Then Mom broke her ankle while stepping off a curb and got prescribed an abnormally large quantity of Vicodin, and I stole it.

The first pill I took happened to kick in right as I sat down to dinner with my family. The relationship between me and Mom had improved ever so slightly after the food court breakdown. But she'd recently started menopausing, which was making her borderline personality thrive and shine, and she was starting to take things out on me again. The specific issue she had with me that night was that I had stopped dressing as sexily as I used to. "You look like you're wearing a tent over your body," she said, motioning to the oversize shirt I was wearing, which came down to my knees and said "Kaiser Permanente" on it. (I will admit, I never took this shirt off. In fact, I referred to it as my "emotional support" shirt because I loved how the softness of its cotton felt on my skin and nipples.) Normally, I would have fought back or internalized this criticism, but I felt so damn happy on Vicodin that I said, "You're right, Mom, I *am* wearing a tent." Then I took the shirt off and ate the remainder of the dinner with my titties out on display.

Vicodin was like Teflon; the critiques didn't stick. They simply rolled right off my body. Its effects didn't only help ease the arguments with Mom. It also helped me to tolerate working a job that I hated. With Vicodin, men's gazes no longer affected me. The fact that Bianca had fucked my first boyfriend didn't affect me, nor did that feeling of constant loneliness that had followed me for years; I actually loved being alone when I was on Vicodin. I didn't even feel a damn thing when Tony Soprano was forced to clip "Big Pussy" Bonpensiero after he'd been flipped. Not even a hint of sadness.

Another cool thing about pills was that the process of stealing them from people's bathrooms provided me with a sense of adventure. At first, that is. My favorite activity was to go to my parents' friends' house and walk straight into their shitters to rummage through their medicine cabinets. Oh, how beautiful and awe-inspiring it was to behold a fully stocked cabinet! You could have offered me a fully paid trip to one of the seven wonders of the world, and I would have turned it down in exchange for a chance to check out your medicine cabinet. Most of the time I came across boring stuff like allergy medication, antidiarrheal and the occasional boner pills, but every now and then I'd hit the narcotic jackpot and acquire myself a few Tylenol with Codeine, a half empty bottle of tramadol, or some expired hydrocodone. The thrill I got while on these missions made me feel like I was Indiana Jones.

On occasions I'd take Vicodin and mix it with alcohol, which caused me to do the strangest shit ever. One time, I had sex with a guy I met while standing at the supermarket checkout and told him I was a virgin, which I wasn't. "Are you sure you want to do this with me?" he asked. "Yes, I want to lose my virginity to you," I answered, then gave him the performance of a lifetime, pretending like I was in pain when he first put it in. When he asked me if I wanted to see him again, I said yes, and gave him Bianca's number. I loved pretending to be a virgin and did it, uh, not infrequently. I guess this was my way of scratching my performance itch? Or maybe it was my way to feel some sort of control over my own life? What a disaster.

Another time, on one of those rare occasions when I left the house and went out to a bar, a guy came up to me and started a conversation. Without thinking or looking at his face, I started talking to him in a fake accent that sounded like a mixture between Penélope Cruz and, I don't know . . . Russian? "Where's your accent from?" he asked. That's when

I got a good look at him and realized how beautiful he was. His name was Beau, and he was tall and thin, with golden skin and black hair that fell over these gorgeous blue eyes.

"I'm from Argentina," I answered. Beau and I dated for six months, during which I never dropped the accent. What was I supposed to do? I had to commit! Sometimes, after spending the night at his place, I'd wake up in the morning and talk in my normal voice, then put the accent back on when I realized I'd fucked up. My friends and parents met him, and I stayed in character the entire time. People thought I was insane. That's because I was insane! I was also addicted to painkillers.

Beau and I broke up because he got into medical school. (He's a rich neurosurgeon now, and I often snoop around his social media, picturing what my life would have been like had we stayed together and wondering if I'd still be speaking in a fake accent.) I wasn't sad about the breakup really. How could I be? I had my Vicodin.

But as it goes with addictions, things eventually stopped being fun (if you can call rummaging through people's bathrooms and being in the loop on which one of my dad's friends took Viagra fun). When I first started taking pills everything felt great: I'd sit down to watch *Mary Poppins* and enjoy it as if it were my first time seeing it, or talk to my family at dinner without getting triggered by every comment my mom made. Eventually, though, the pills turned me into a dumbfuck. I'd take them, lose track of time, and stare off into the void catatonically for hours with no idea of what was going on around me. I was on a delay. Nilda would ask me what I wanted her to make for dinner, and I'd answer her two days later.

One time I lit myself on fire. I was standing next to the stove, wearing a robe, when one of the sleeves went up in flames. I didn't even notice until a few seconds later when Nilda ran into the kitchen and started screaming and dragged me into the swimming pool. On another occasion I got on the freeway and started driving south when I meant to drive north. I didn't realize I'd been driving in the opposite direction until an hour into the drive. I once drove through a red light and got a ticket in the mail. It included a photo of me that was taken at the exact moment in which I was crossing the red light. Man, did I look zonked out, holding a cigarette out the window, with my eyes half closed. I bet you I was listening to Enya's "Orinoco Flow" while it was taken. I listened to that song on repeat back then.

Eventually the bliss of being fucked up faded, and I entered a state of perpetual irritability. I didn't want people to talk to me, and I was annoyed at the sight of my own face. Plus, my stash started to run low, so I found myself breaking my pills in half and then in quarters to make them last longer. I no longer had the luxury of taking a pill every day, so I started spacing them out. I stopped taking them to go to work, which made me incredibly annoyed with the patients I interpreted for, especially when they'd ramble on instead of giving me straight answers.

Then, one particularly shitty morning that I'll never live down, I was driving to work when I decided that I'd make an exception and take something because that day I'd be interpreting for a doctor who was a gargantuan piece of shit. A few months earlier, while interpreting for him, he asked me to come into his office because he wanted to "teach me some exercises that would be good for my posture." After I followed him in, he closed the door and he asked me to stand straight against a wall. He pulled my shoulders back to show me what good posture looked like, and then just fully cupped and jiggled both my breasts for like ten seconds. "That should help with your posture," he said. "Thanks," I answered, confused because I'd never, not once, complained to him about my posture and also . . . what the fuck?

After this incident, the doctor pretended like nothing happened, and so did I. For a couple of weeks I was in denial that he'd fondled my titties, and I actually convinced myself that the man was really trying to help my posture. I considered not returning, but I made good money whenever I worked with him, so I accepted another job. While driving to this festering shit pipe of a man's office, I thought I'd take something that would help me numb out in case he acted like a creep again. I knew I had a half pill loose somewhere in the bottom of my bag, so I reached in there and felt around. There it was! My little chunk of a pill! As I pulled it out, however, it slipped out of my hand, falling somewhere under my seat. I reached down to try to reach it, taking my eyes off the road for a second. And then, something violently exploded in my face.

The first thing I saw when I opened my eyes and came to my senses was a large, ten-foot Buzz Lightyear smiling at me. He may even have been giving me the thumbs-up. I then heard people screaming as they ran up to my car to make sure I was alive and realized I'd crashed into an L.A. city bus. I was going forty miles per hour and looked down when I slammed right into the back of it while it was stopped at a bus stop, waiting for all the morning commuters to load in. It happened to be advertising a billboard for the latest *Toy Story* movie.

Wanna know what the worst part of all this was? The first thought that ran through my head wasn't "I hope I didn't kill anyone" but "I hope I can find that pill I dropped."

A Parade of Deaths

My accident brought with it a whole bunch of crapola, all of which I completely deserved. This included a totaled car, a large amount of shame, guilt, and embarrassment, of course, a disgusting increase in my car insurance premium (it went from fifty dollars to four hundred dollars a month), and a back injury that continues to bother me today. No one else was hurt, thank god. But I do want to give myself a (painful) pat on the back, because I took the car accident as the warning sign that it was and decided to stop with the pain pills and the weed. A great decision, right? Right. Except I took it a step too far and thought, "if I'm going to get clean, let's go all the way," and stopped taking the antidepressants as well.

For the first month, I suffered what I refer to as "brain zaps." This is what happens when you stop taking antidepressants from one day to the next, without tapering off. It basically makes you feel like your brain is being electrocuted for twenty or so seconds. Like you've just been kicked in the head by a mule. During these brain zaps, you lose your vision and balance and are just kind of left there, wobbling and confused.

The absence of the narcotics caused me to suffer from a horrible case of restless leg syndrome. I looked like I was one of the fucking Riverdance dancers. I also couldn't sleep, had night sweats, and cried at literally *everything*. Suddenly, all the emotions I'd denied myself in the previous year squirted out of me uncontrollably. I was a broken fire hydrant of emotions and tears. I cried watching a toilet paper commercial, in which the Charmin bear taught a smaller bear (who I assumed was his son) how to wipe his ass. It was so beautiful. I cried if someone honked their horn at me, or if the drive-thru line at McDonald's was too long. I cried while looking at a bag of chicharrón because I got sad for the pigs.

A lot of this crying took place in front of my family, who didn't understand that I was crying because the drugs were leaving my body and figured I was just sensitive because the car crash had shaken me up. More than once I had to excuse myself from the dinner table because I'd start getting emotional. "Remember Aida Pfefferman? She ran the hair salon near my apartment on Corrientes? She died today. She had cancer of the vulva," Nilda said one day at dinner, in a tone that I found to be completely lacking in empathy.

"You hear of ovarian cancer or uterine cancer, but cancer in the vulva!? I've never heard of such a thing!" Mom answered nonchalantly.

"I knew a guy who had cancer on his hemorrhoid," Dad chimed in.

"Can you guys please have more respect for human beings!?" I screamed at them, running away from the table and locking myself in my room to cry. Because I *did* remember Aida Pfefferman, the lady who ran the hair salon near Nilda's apartment. She was always so nice to me when I came in to get my bangs cut during my childhood. She had this special skill where she could gleek on command, and it made me laugh. And now she was dead!

And then, as my nervous system began getting its groove back and I was starting to bask in the freedom of not being beholden to a bottle of prescription pills, we received the news that my grandpa Pocho died. Pocho's passing didn't come as a surprise. In the months prior to his death, he'd been in and out of the hospital because his lungs were filling up with fluid and his heart was giving out. Ever since we moved to the United States, I'd made it a point to talk to Pocho on the phone at least once a week. When I graduated from high school and went backpacking through Europe with Meg, I made sure to call Pocho from every city I visited.

"My friend did too many drugs and won't leave the hostel. I don't know what to do," I told him after Meg took mushrooms, ecstasy, *and* morphine on our first night in Amsterdam and proceeded to sleep for forty-eight hours straight.

"Fuck your friend," Pocho advised me. "Do your grandpa a favor. Drink a glass of whiskey and go to the red-light district in search of the best pair of melons you can find."

"Why not?" I answered him, then headed out into the night.

Sometimes I called Pocho but didn't have much to say to him. So, instead of talking, I played him my favorite songs over the phone and listened to him hum along. There was one specific song he liked, which he asked me to play for him over and over again: "Constant Craving" by k.d. lang (which turns out to be about samsara, the Buddhist cycle of life and death).

Mom called to tell me that Pocho had passed right as I was about to go on my lunch break while translating at an orthopedic clinic. I'm so grateful that I was sober to process his death. When I got the news, I was compelled to do something I hadn't done in a long, long time: perform. I didn't do it in front of a crowd or get on a stage. It wasn't that kind of performance. I sat in my car, alone, in the middle of a parking lot, and sang "Constant Craving," just for him. I sang so intensely and with so much emotion inside that car that I felt like I was Celine Dion, Luciano Pavarotti, and Chaka Khan all wrapped into one. And then, when the song ended and I came out of my stupor, I realized that Deanna, the megabutch X-ray technician from the office (who actually looked a lot like k.d. lang now that I think about it) had been standing in the parking lot watching me sing this lesbian anthem at the top of my lungs.

Pocho died on September 28. Freakishly, my mom and her mother, Rita, were born on that same day, September 28. But it gets weirder. One year after Pocho's passing, my aunt Sandra, who had been living with my grandma Rita in Buenos Aires in what appeared to have turned into a Grey Gardens situation of mother-daughter codependency and abuse, woke up one morning and started coughing up blood. She was only in her fifties, but she smoked so many cigarettes her fingertips had started turning yellow from the nicotine. Sandra stopped taking her medication and started spending her time roaming the streets and getting drunk in a decrepit pool hall bar. The only silver lining to her sad and shitty life was that, days after her cough started, she went in for a biopsy and died on the operating table without finding out that she also had been suffering from an untreatable stage four lung cancer. Guess what day she died? September 28.

Now that Sandra was dead, Rita, who was in her eighties, was alone and unable to care for herself. Our choices were to put her in a geriatric home in Buenos Aires and let her live out her remaining years in total solitude, or bring her to the United States and let her live out her remaining years with us, her family who loved her dearly. Just kidding—not a single one of us was jumping for joy at the idea of her moving in. The woman was one cold cunt, after all. But Mom couldn't bear the idea of letting her die alone, so we put her on a plane and brought her to the United States. I was now twenty-seven years old, and not only still living at home with my parents, but with both of my grandmothers as well.

When Rita moved in with us, she seemed different. She was still kind of cunty, of course, but there was a fun sassiness to her that I'd never noticed when she was around Pocho. It was as if, without him around, she came to life and developed an identity of her own. I actually enjoyed her company. We watched a lot of TV together: gossip shows, Turkish soap operas, horror films. One time I made her watch my favorite movie with me, John Waters's *Pink Flamingos*, and she fucking loved it, specifically the part where Divine shoplifts a raw steak by shoving it in her crotch.

"Your generation is a degenerate mess," she said, laughing and pointing her crooked, arthritic finger at the TV.

"This movie was made in the early seventies, Rita. That's *your* generation, not mine," I answered, laughing with her.

Something else that changed in Rita, now that Pocho was gone, was that she wanted to eat. I have no prior memories of Rita eating. In fact, many times, I'd overheard her say that her biggest fear in life was to get as fat as Nilda. Nilda wasn't an idiot. She knew that Rita prided herself on being the thin grandmother. So now that the two of them were living together, and Rita was finally allowing herself to eat, Nilda, who controlled the kitchen, enacted revenge on her by refusing to cook for her. Whereas I felt total joy in making this starved woman whatever she wanted. I was no cook, though, so I could offer her only a limited menu consisting of sandwiches and quesadillas.

"Bring me a ham and cheese sandwich, and make sure it's dripping with mayonnaise," she'd yell at me from across the room.

"Yes, Goddess," I'd answer. I don't know why, but I had started referring to her as goddess when she moved in with us. Of course, she fucking loved it (the woman was a narcissist, after all). I'd present her with a decadent sandwich on a silver tray and she'd devour it like it was her last meal on Earth. She'd then let me know she was finished and I could come pick up the tray by letting out an earthquake-size burp that could be heard across the house.

Rita, who was the one grandparent of mine who never played with me or asked me questions about myself, was suddenly interested in knowing everything about me.

"Tell me about all the beefcakes you've slept with," she said as I tucked her in one night. I'd then sit at the foot of her bed and tell her about this French guy I had sex with who loved to jerk off while smelling my armpits, or about this musician I used to hook up with back in my record label days whose penis curved dramatically to the left and always begged me to lick his asshole.

"Did you lick it?" she asked, completely bewildered by what she was hearing.

"Of course I did, Goddess. It tasted like toilet paper." I answered.

"That's disgusting. Who knew my granddaughter would turn out to be one big slut?" she replied, breaking into a contagious laughter. Seconds later, she got quiet, however, and added, "I should have enjoyed my life and had sex with other men. Your grandfather did whatever the hell he wanted."

Even though Rita seemed to be thriving mentally, her physical condition was a disaster. The woman was literally rotting in front of our eyes. She looked three hundred years old. This is really disgusting, even for me, so skip over the next few sentences if you're easily grossed out, but she had this smell emanating from her crotch that was so putrid it made us gag whenever we had to change her diapers. That smell was no joke. It was as if a skunk had died, rotted, and then been sprayed with fish sauce (I'm so sorry). I have no idea what it was caused by, but I can still smell it more than ten years later. Rita was barely mobile by this point, so we'd just sit her on a big recliner where she'd stay all day until it was time to transfer her to bed. As a matter of fact, the one time she tried to get up on her own, only a couple of weeks after moving in with us, she fell and broke her hip and had to be rushed to the hospital for an emergency hip replacement.

"I haven't slept that well in years," she mumbled on awakening from the anesthesia. Dad immediately leaned over and whispered in her ear.

"Rita, listen to me carefully. You *do not* have health insurance in the United States. That means your family, meaning us, are responsible for your hospital bills. So, whatever you do, *do not* tell anyone at this hospital that we're related to you." Rita looked up at us, still high out of her mind. But she totally understood what he was saying to her.

"These people are not my family. They're my friends . . . from temple," she screamed loud enough for the hospital billing person to hear. She then motioned to Nilda, who was sitting near the bed and took a nice little jab at her by adding, "Except for her, I don't know that ugly woman," before falling back asleep.

Approximately seventy thousand dollars in unpaid medical bills later, Rita was released from the hospital and allowed to return to our home with a giant stash of painkillers, which were stored in my bathroom and which I came *extremely* close to stealing. On numerous occasions, I opened that beautiful bottle of hydrocodone, put a few pills in my hand, and just let them rest there for a few seconds before putting them back where they belonged. I was being tested. But I believe that the reason I always ended up putting the pills back was because I was . . . happy? I sort of thrived off the chaos of living at home with my parents and my two intense grandmothers. The house felt full in a good way. Full of family, which reminded me of my life in Argentina.

This happiness can be attributed to the fact that I was starting to feel creatively fulfilled again. My car-singing tribute to Pocho led to other avenues of self-expression. I learned how to speak French and began piano lessons. I started writing daily, filling up journals with every thought that crossed my mind. During my translating jobs, I'd write down everything

I witnessed in the waiting rooms: the patients snoring, the filthy fish tank with dead fish floating inside it, the receptionist sitting behind her desk eating Hot Cheetos with chopsticks to avoid dirtying her gem-encrusted acrylics. But mostly I wrote about all the things that were going on at home. I even signed up for a creative writing class at my local junior college. During that class I wrote a one-act play about Rita and Nilda's ongoing feud called "I Can't Wait for You to Die," and a short story titled "The Grandmother" about a dumb guy who kidnaps some millionaire's grandmother and asks for a ransom in exchange for her. The grandmother (whose character was loosely based on Rita) is a demanding woman who is so good at picking on her kidnapper's deepest insecurities that she leads him to commit suicide before he manages to collect the ransom money. It was published in the school newspaper.

Rita's health declined severely when she came home from the hospital. She was starting to slip mentally as well as physically. During the day, she was mostly motionless and vacant. But the moment the rest of us would try to go to sleep, she'd start having conversations with dead people. She'd lie in bed talking to Sandra in particular for hours. Sometimes she got so angry. She'd reproach her deceased daughter, saying things like, "I'll never forgive you for marrying a goy." Other times, she'd apologize to her for neglecting her as a child. "I'm so sorry, Sandra. Let me in," she'd beg. "Please, let me in."

Now, as I've previously mentioned, my family has always been very open when it came to sex. This means that the entire time I lived at home with them, they were totally okay with my bringing guys over and never gave me shit for locking myself in my room with some random dude that none of us would ever see again. One night, I brought over this guy I'd met while smoking a cigarette outside my creative writing class. Me and the guy were hooking up in my bedroom, which was adjacent to Rita's, and as he was going down on me, all I could focus on was the fact that my dying grandma was ripping farts while having a tea party with her dead family members. "What beautiful chinaware you have, Trudy," she said to her cousin Gertrude, who had died like forty years ago after getting run over by a car. "I'll take a droplet of milk with my tea, Aunt Maria," she said to some other ghost while this man tried his hardest to make me cum. It was so distracting and grotesque that I made him stop and went into her bedroom to try to bring her back to reality.

"Goddess! Wake up. You're entering a different dimension again," I said, trying to bring her back to the earthly realm.

"Would you like a macaroon?" she responded, then handed me an invisible treat she'd plucked from thin air.

One morning Rita woke up and asked me to get Mom for her, because she wanted to tell her something important. Totally clear-headed, she informed Mom that she hated my grandfather Pocho because he'd been a horrible husband and had cheated on her their entire marriage. "He ruined my life and I'm glad he's dead. I hope he burns in hell," she told Mom, who didn't believe her and assumed it was the dementia talking. Rita then asked us to take her to the bathroom so she could look at herself in the mirror. "Wow, I'm old," she said, taking in her reflection. "I look like absolute shit and it's time for me to die," she added. We laid her back down in her bed and she ordered one final sandwich from me. She ate it in silence and, halfway through, looked at me and said in her incredible, cunty voice that I had become totally obsessed with, "This sandwich is too dry. Not enough mayonnaise." Then her face turned blue, and Mom and I watched her die.

Moments later, while Mom was in the other room having a complete meltdown over the fact that her entire family was dead and she was now an orphan, I got into bed with Rita and held her dead body. I brushed her hair with my fingers, observed the bruises on her hands that were left over from the IV she'd been given at the hospital, and then, for some reason, I was compelled to grab her arm and start sucking on her elbow. I know it's weird, but I wanted to take it all in and, sometimes, taking it all in means sucking on a dead person's elbow. I don't know what I expected a dead person's elbow to taste like, but it tasted sweeter than anything else I've ever tasted in my entire life.

After Rita's death, we had a few months where life returned to its usual pace. Although, I have to admit, I did miss the chaos that my Goddess brought to the house. During this time I made a point to give Nilda all the attention I hadn't been able to give her while Rita was with us. I watched her cook and asked her to teach me how to make her famous Waldorf salad that I loved so much. I floated in the pool with her. I even attended a potluck at the English class she was taking at some adult school where I heard her sing John Lennon's "Imagine" as her final presentation. That evening Nilda came home showing off a certificate stating that she'd graduated from level one English class. She was so proud of herself, she asked Dad if he'd frame it for her. She then went on one of her nightly walks around the neighborhood. When she returned, she complained to Dad that she had difficulty breathing. Dad went to get her some water, but by the time he got back, Nilda was drenched in a cold sweat and attempting to remove her clothes because she couldn't breathe. Before Dad could get to a phone to call 911, she'd begun foaming at the mouth. Less than a minute later, she had died from a massive heart attack, in the same bedroom where Rita had died just a few months earlier.

I happened to be at the movies when this death took place. When I came home and found out what had happened, I was overcome with an insane hunger. Up until now, every time I'd lost a grandparent or a loved one, my grief was accompanied by a total loss of appetite. But with Nilda's death, for some reason I felt the opposite. While everyone wept, I rummaged through the fridge, desperate to find any leftover food Nilda had left behind. In the back of the fridge, I found a dozen empanadas she had made for us a few days before, and I ate the shit out of them while I sobbed and stared at her graduation certificate, which Dad had just hung up for her on our kitchen wall. I then realized that Nilda, who had never had any formal schooling whatsoever, had managed to graduate from her first class ever on the very day of her death.

The following week, we cremated her body and buried her next to Rita in a nearby cemetery. In attendance were us, the Moldavskys, and a few other Argentines, including a rabbi friend of theirs who was constantly reminding people about the importance of keeping kosher, but whom I once caught devouring pork sausages over the kitchen sink when he thought no one was watching. During the service, a line from Gabriel García Márquez's *One Hundred Years of Solitude* popped into my head. "A person does not belong to a place until there is someone dead under the ground." I guess this meant that I finally belonged.

When we came home from the burial, I looked around the house where both my grandmothers had died. A house that not long ago had been filled with grandmothers and laughter and fighting and cooking. A house that had been full of Argentina, but now felt completely silent and desolate. And suddenly I was taken back to those miserable years when we moved to the United States. The silence was so overwhelming and loud that it started ringing in my ears. I walked to my bathroom, opened my medicine cabinet, and did the one thing that I knew would make me feel better: take one of the pain pills Rita had left behind. I then went straight to the pool and floated face-down on Nilda's favorite floating device that was shaped like a pink shell. As the pill kicked in, I stuck my head underwater, holding my breath for as long as I could, until I felt like my lungs were going to collapse. I knew that if I stayed in that house, I'd go right back to taking pills. It was time for me to move out.

Failed Child Star

Six months after Nilda's death, when I was close to turning thirty, I finally moved out of my parents' house in Orange County and into my first apartment in downtown Los Angeles. It was my first time living on my own, and by "on my own" I mean that I moved out with my sister. My sister and I had always been close, but we were never friends per se. This changed, however, as the two of us got older and I stopped seeing her as my little sister. If only I would have realized, during my loneliest years, that I had a built-in best friend the entire time.

As we got closer, my sister and I didn't just share a trip through our mother's vaginal canal as well as a bunch of trips back and forth from Argentina to the United States, we started sharing friends, clothes, and, at times, we even shared men. It wasn't as weird as it sounds. It was more like if I hooked up with a guy who I knew wasn't for me, I'd be like "you should meet my sister." I guess that is kind of weird now that I put it on paper. But by the time we moved out, we had a list of men we'd handed over to each other and whom we'd given nicknames like "Guy-who-wears-baby-powder-on-his-balls," "receding-gums-guy," or "guy-who-makes-too-many-jokes-about-wanting-to-stab-people."

We weren't the only ones who left the suburbs. A few months after my sister and I moved out, my parents lost the Disneyland account and their food truck business started to tank. According to them, the person who is to blame for this is . . . Magic Johnson. Turns out, he owns a company that provides food to the cafeterias that feed all the Disneyland employees, and when said company realized that there was a competing food truck feeding the workers and taking most of their business, they had my parents kicked out. Now, I don't think Magic Johnson was the one who made the decision to have my parents removed from Disneyland. But Mom does. She thinks Earvin got word of how well they were doing, and how they were taking his business, and got on the phone and said "get the Argentines out of here." I told her that it probably wasn't him and that he's got bigger fish to fry, but she wouldn't have it. She continues to this day to harbor a gigantic grudge against Magic Johnson. His name cannot even be spoken in her presence. Magic Johnson is the man who shall not be named.

The loss of the Disneyland account led my parents to file for bankruptcy, after which they lost everything they owned, including the house of their American dreams with the swimming pool where both my grandmothers died. Luckily, the devastation that my parents felt about losing everything they'd ever worked for was quickly replaced with a sense of excitement about changing up their lives and following their daughters to the city. So without hesitation, they gave up the house and rented a cheap, hipster-y loft in the middle of downtown Los Angeles, exactly two blocks away from where my sister and I lived.

Moving to L.A. changed my life. Even though I continued working as an interpreter, I was living in a neighborhood that was full of art galleries and music venues, and I started meeting so many creative people. There was Hannah, a bombshell with high cheekbones and a pixie haircut who had an obsession with roosters. "Roosters are a symbol of courage," she told me the day we met at a house party where a punk band was playing for an audience that consisted of Shia LaBeouf, a fifty-year-old drunk Russian guy who claimed to have been in the band Rush, and a bunch of people dressed like clowns.

A few days after we met, Hannah invited me to her house where I witnessed her abnormal collection of ceramic rooster figurines. There were thousands of them! That day she told me she'd recently started an all-girl band which she'd named Raaats (the band name "Rooosters" was already taken, so she'd named the band after her second-favorite animal).

"You should join," she said. "Do you play any instruments?" My instant reaction was to say no. The thought of getting on a stage truly just felt impossible. I simply didn't have the balls. Sure, in the last few years I'd done things like sing a song in my car for my dead grandfather, but other than that, I had mostly repressed that side of myself because I associated it with shame and failure.

"We sound like complete shit, but it's fun," she added. There was something about the ease with which Hannah talked about performing that made it feel easy and not loaded with fraught emotional shit. I looked around the room at the hundreds of hideous and courageous little roosters, and I accepted.

"Fuck it, why not? I can play keys and I can sing backups," I answered, remembering that I had, in fact, taken piano lessons a few years back, but had never actually played in front of anyone. And then I said something that I don't think I had ever said out loud in my entire adult life: "You know, I actually used to be a child star."

A few months later, when Raaats played a show at a venue by the name of The Smell, I met Fran, the drummer for one of the headlining bands that night. She was a Jewish New Yorker with a theater background, eighteen day jobs, and a get-shit-done, type A attitude that will accomplish ten tasks during the time it takes you to release one fart. Fran said that she organized readings in her apartment, so when I mentioned that I'd written a few short plays and stories, she signed me up.

The next weekend, I got up in front of a crowd in her apartment and read a monologue I'd written titled "Young Slut." It told the story of a girl who'd just performed her first blow job and was based on my teenage years of underage clubbing during which I was, well, a young slut. I read the entire piece in an exaggerated, Valley girl accent while sipping on a giant 7/11 Big Gulp cup, which I'd brought as a prop. The monologue went something like:

> On a scale of one to ten, one being that you're a terrible dick sucker and ten being that you're a porn star, like super professional, and can moan and suck the penis at

the same time, I'd probably rate my first blow job at a six. The problem was I think I kept scraping the sides of his penis with my teeth. Well, I don't <u>think</u> I scraped it, I definitely scraped it because he kept saying, "Owww, teeth. Owww teeth."

People were crying with laughter. "Where can we see you perform again?" they asked me at the end of the night. I looked over at Fran, who was chewing on her tongue (which I came to learn is what she did while she plotted something in her head), and she was, as a matter of fact, putting together a production in her mind. At the end of the night, she walked up to me and said, "I need you to write a few more monologues like the one you just read. I'm going to direct you in a one-woman show."

A few months later I walked out onto the stage of a black box theater to perform "Cumming of Age," a forty-five-minute play written and performed by me and directed by Fran made up of monologues in which I played four women in different stages of their life: a little girl, a teenager, a middle-aged woman, and an old lady. These four characters were based on my own life experiences, but also inspired by traits from all the women in my life. They were a little of Mom, Rita, Nilda, Bubaleh, Sandra, my sister, and Meg, who had moved back to California after a couple of cocaine-fueled years selling timeshares in Cancun.

As I bowed for a sold-out theater full of people who loved me, I thought, "I'm so fucking proud of myself right now, if a truck runs me over and kills me, I'd be okay with it."

Shortly after the play, I got a call from Bianca Moldavsky (who'd recently graduated from law school) informing me that she was also moving to Los Angeles. In the last few years, Bianca had gotten a lot of work done: three nose jobs, boob implants, lips like sausages, and as many fillers as her face could tolerate without exploding. The woman looked like a bloated calzone. Bianca didn't know many people in the city, so, like an idiot, I made a point of introducing her to all my new friends who (thankfully) hated her instantly. I invited her to a Raaats show at an Irish pub where she stood in the back in her tight, bodycon dress and hair extensions with a sour look on her face. I also invited her to a few dinner parties where each guest was supposed to prepare a dish, and Bianca refused to eat the dish of anyone who looked poor. My friends never understood why I kept inviting her out. "She's like a cousin to me," I'd say, excusing her off-putting behavior.

Then one day her grandma Dorita (the one who refused to give me rides when I first got to this country) died, and I didn't call Bianca to say I was sorry for her loss. To put it simply, I just didn't fucking feel like it. A few days later, I got a call from Bianca. She sounded pissed.

"How dare you not call me to say you're sorry that my grandmother died," she said, scolding me over the phone. Might I add that she never called me when *my* grandma died. She kept going. "You think you're so cool now with your new little L.A. friends. You know what you are? You're a bad, bad friend." I was stunned, but what's weird is I also found myself agreeing with her. This is what happens after years of having someone make you feel like you're lesser than them. You start to believe everything they say.

"I'm really sorry, Bianca," I answered. "I should have been there for you. Let me make it up to you and take you to lunch tomorrow."

The moment I hung up the phone, I felt nothing but rage and hatred running through my veins. I was so angry I grabbed a vase from a shelf and smashed it against the wall, causing my sister to run out of her room. I picked up the phone again and called Bianca back.

"What's up?" she answered.

"Listen to me, you little cunty bitch. You make me sick. How dare you fucking lecture me about being a good friend? I should have told you to eat shit back in the day when you made fun of me and called me a F.O.B., and then again when you fucked my boyfriend. But I didn't, so I'm going to go ahead and do it now. Please, do me a huge favor and go fuck yourself you absolute piece of shit." I then hung up the phone and looked back at my sister.

"Who were you just talking to?" she asked.

"Bianca Moldavsky," I answered.

"Good for you," she said. And you know what? It *was* good for me. I should have had the balls to do this when I was younger. But a wise man (that I made up in my mind just now) once said to me: "Everyone's balls drop on their own time." And I guess this was the day when my little rounds finally dropped.

Ever since that call, no one in my family has spoken to the Moldavskys. Even my parents, who had a friendship with them of more than twenty years. I think that final phone call between Bianca and me made things really weird for all of them. Plus, by the end, my parents simply got kind of sick of their snootiness. In the present, we have all mutually blocked each other on every single social media platform, even LinkedIn.

I dream about the Moldavskys all the time. In my dreams I don't feel animosity toward them. On the contrary, I'm always happy to see them. But then, when I wake up, you know what makes me even happier than the fact that I saw them in the dream? The fact that I don't have to deal with them ever again as long as I live. I guess the Moldavskys were like family, and you're not always bound to like your family. And they did help us when we first moved to the States. But all the help came with a price. For example, if Mom and Dad made new friends, they always had to be vetted by the Moldavskys, and my parents always had to be grateful to them and at their mercy. The truth is, they were judgmental snobs, and we were just different kinds of people. I've learned that that's something immigrants are commonly faced with, forced friendships with people you wouldn't normally be friends with just because you come from the same country. This wasn't just true about my parents. It's the exact reason why I forced a friendship with Bianca. She was an Argentinian girl my age in a place where there were no Argentinian girls.

Once the Moldavskys were out of our lives, my parents seemed to relax and make new friends without worrying about being judged. They developed a bit of a new identity, just as Rita had after Pocho died. In fact, my mom did something she never would have done if she were still friends with the Moldavskys: she started an OnlyFans page! One day, a friend of hers mentioned that she had a great body and would probably make a good amount of money on OnlyFans.

"What is Only Funs?" she called to ask me later that day.

"Only Funs?" I answered.

"Only Funs. Where you post pictures naked for money."

"OnlyFans! Do you want to start an OnlyFans?" I said, shocked, but not really shocked, to be honest. When I was a child star, my mom lived vicariously through me. Now she'd get all the attention herself. She'd be fulfilling a narcissist dream.

"Yes. Can you help me set up a page? My friend says I can post pictures of my feet and make millions of dollars," she said.

A few years later, as in the present day, Mom (aka "Hot Argentina Mami") has a thriving OnlyFans page with hundreds of followers including my sister and me, who subscribed to her page with very creative fake names like Ricardo and Roberto so that she wouldn't recognize us. What can I say? We want to support Mom's endeavors. And sure, she doesn't make millions of dollars like she was expecting, but she makes enough to get her nails done every month and to cover part of the mortgage of a cheap fixer-upper that they bought and Dad remodeled himself (he is an architect, after all). Anyway, Mom doesn't *just* post feet pics. Showing only her feet got boring and was too limiting. She wanted to express herself fully, fully nude. Also, she was insecure about the bunion on her right foot, which men most definitely jerked off to, but which she said was ugly and red like a clown's nose. Currently, you can find lots of classic titty shots, sexy shots of her bending over in bed wearing lingerie, and a few videos of her showering. Mom looks fucking amazing. Good for her.

The best part of her business is that it's a family affair. Dad takes her photos and is the art director. For President's Day, for example, he asked me to print out the faces of a few American presidents. He then taped the faces to the wall and took pictures of her, in an American flag shirt, bending over in front of them. Admittedly, sometimes you can tell he's lazy and does a half-ass job with the pictures. Like, you can see him in a few of them, reflected in the mirror, wearing shorts and no shirt. Other times you can spot one of their extremely overweight dogs, Titty and Pussy, in the background of a shot. (Those are the dogs' actual names, but when I take them to the vet, I say their names are Lucy and Ethel to spare myself the embarrassment.) My sister does a lot of Mom's styling, and I'm in charge of writing her copy. The tagline I wrote for her is as follows: "Mother of two. Proud of my body. 100% prime Argentinian meat." I also help with some other creative stuff. One time I suggested that she start selling used panties for fifty dollars a pair. She made six hundred dollars. Not bad! Another time a man messaged her asking her to record a video of herself where she insulted him.

"What should I say to him?" she asked me.

"Well. You can insult the size of his balls perhaps," I answered.

"Men like that?"

"Some men get horny if you insult them."

"Ohhh. I didn't know that," she said, genuinely shocked.

"Why don't you say something like: You're a disgusting freak and you have a tiny scrotum that looks like a half-eaten peanut," I suggested.

"That's too complicated for me to say in English," she answered.

"Okay then, maybe something like. Your balls and dick look like shit," I said.

"Perfect."

As for me, I continued working as a translator for a few more years until I got a job working for the famous eighties girl band the Bangles. A good friend of mine happened to be Susanna Hoffs's niece and told me they were looking for someone to help them with scheduling, emails, styling, and the occasional tour managing. When I met Susanna, we clicked right away, and she became a close friend and mentor. One weekend, I accompanied her to the Rock & Roll Hall of Fame in New York because she'd been asked to introduce the Zombies. She and I were sitting at a table at the after-party (where I got to meet Robert Smith and Stevie Nicks) when I told Susanna all about my days in Argentina as a child star, and how I stripped down to a garter belt while impersonating Madonna at Hebraica. I told her about my years at the record label, about Raaats and how we'd be filming our first music video in the coming weeks. And she looked at me and said, "Performing just keeps making its way into your life in one form or another, doesn't it? You should write about your life." Then Susanna and I were approached by a really nice man with curly hair who looked vaguely familiar. As he walked up to us, he mistakenly stepped on my toes. He apologized profusely and said, "Where is your accent from?"

"I'm from Argentina," I answered.

"Argentina! One of my favorite places in the world," he said. I still couldn't place him, until Susanna leaned over and whispered in my ear.

"That's Brian May, from Queen."

I eventually took Susanna's advice and sat down to write a TV pilot about a young girl who was a star in Argentina and after immigrating to the United States with her family attempted to become the child star she once was and failed. She now found herself abusing pain pills because she felt unfulfilled working a job as a Spanish translator and living with her unfiltered parents who openly spoke about poop and sex. I truly do not remember writing it. I didn't know how to write a TV show. I'd never even read a single TV script. I swear to you I blacked out, and the story just poured out of me. When it was finished, I sent it to a friend who worked as a producer who, in turn, sent it to a few managers. My story didn't click with most of these Hollywood types. "I'm going to be transparent with you," one manager said to me, "the story just doesn't feel real to me. And why are the parents so disgusting?" After I'd given up on it, I got an email from a manager telling me he'd really connected with my pilot. "Let's send it out to people and see what happens," he told me.

Within months, I started getting meetings with showrunners who were responding to my script and looking to staff me on TV shows. The first show I made it on was Apple's *Acapulco*. On my first day of work, it hit me that I had absolutely no idea how writers' rooms worked. I knew the showrunner was the boss (because I googled it), but I didn't know there was a hierarchy of writers that ranged from staff writer, the lowest level (me), to producers and executive producers. I had no idea how "pitching" worked, how important story and character arcs were. I went in there completely blind. But all the change I've had to deal with throughout my life came in handy. It made me adaptable and observant. Above all, I was so fucking happy and grateful to be there. I was no longer working in hospitals, repeating what other people said all day. I was getting paid to be creative.

I eventually staffed on my second show, Hulu's *This Fool*, which I think is one of the funniest, weirdest, and most perfect shows out there. I can't explain how much I laughed during that writers' room, telling anecdotes about shitting my pants, sucking on my grandma's elbow, or pitching storylines about rabbits with giant penises. I often say to myself, "It's not normal to be this happy about going to work." It's when I have those joyful realizations that the fear that the rug will be pulled out from under me sets in. That's the pattern I became accustomed to throughout my youth: If something good happens, it will probably be taken from me. And that's something I just have to get over.

Ultimately, writing allowed me to feel creatively fulfilled, without people's gazes being placed on me in a way that made me feel vulnerable. Performing is still very much a part of my life. I eventually formed a second band called Moded. I hosted podcasts and comedy shows. But as much as I still enjoy getting on stages, I prefer pitching stories about a girl who once did the splits and broke her pussy, and then seeing those stories come to life on television.

One day, I got a call from my manager, letting me know that Selena Gomez had read my pilot and wanted to attach herself as an executive producer on it. From one day to the next I found myself prepping to pitch the show to various streamers who were interested in buying it. It really felt like a dream. Two former child stars working together on a show about the difficulties and pressures of being a child star: One who had succeeded, and one who had failed, kind of. Actually, I hadn't failed at all.

The morning of my pitch, I was overcome with a level of nerves that I'd never experienced in my entire life. I had explosive diarrhea that just wouldn't stop, and I was shaking so hard I could barely hold a glass of water without dropping it. I was a fucking mess. It felt as if every moment of my entire life had led up to this one. Selling this show wouldn't just change my life, it would potentially change my family's life as well. And that was a lot of pressure. So I did something that in the past had helped me get through tough situations (no, not Vicodin). I closed my eyes and traveled to another place, just like I used to do in my days of dissociating after we'd moved back to Argentina. I went into *Torokoooo, Sureteeee, Bondidichiiii Shokamamaaaa* mode. This time, I imagined myself floating down Avenida Corrientes. I started at El Obelisco and floated down theater row, past the auditorium where Pocho and I saw the *My Little Pony* musical, where my balloon floated away. I floated across the fabric district and saw the beauty salon that Rita once took me to watch her get her roots retouched. I passed Conchita's studio, and the ethereal jacaranda trees that lined the sidewalks. I made my way into Villa Crespo, the Jewish neighborhood where Nilda and Benjamín lived. I crossed the intersection where my mother's water broke, where she turned back to my grandparents to call them "a bunch of pieces of shit." I then floated back to the United States, hovering above the food court where people lined up by the hundreds to get a taste of Sexy Chicken's poultry delights, and that other food court where Mom and I had our big blowout after we'd been granted our green cards. Finally, I returned to my body, calmly got ready, and headed into my pitch.

Four years, a pandemic, seven staffing jobs on TV shows, two bands, and a marriage later, I find myself on the balcony of my great-aunt Chichi's penthouse overlooking Buenos Aires, smoking a cigarette alone to calm the buzz and emotions. This hasn't been my first trip back to Argentina. (I returned once in the early 2000s, after we received our green cards, but I was accompanied by Bianca, and we spent the entire trip clubbing until five in the morning and then sleeping all day. I also returned with my mom so that we could bury Sandra. I spent a total of seventy-two hours in the country, most of it in a hospital, a morgue, and a funeral home.) This time my return feels real. I'm back in Argentina for the first time as a grown woman with a successful writing career, and I'm taking it all in.

I'm full of red wine and cold cuts, because I know that Pocho is keeping tally from the afterlife of how many salamis I eat, and I want to make my grandpa proud. I also have a zit on the side of my nose the size of a soccer ball, which I attribute to all the dulce de leche I've consumed in the past week I've been back in the country. Other than the acne, I feel fucking amazing. I had my cell phone stolen yesterday while standing outside Nilda's old apartment on Calle Corrientes. I noticed a FOR SALE sign on her old living room window (where Mom sliced Nilda's arm with a knife) and started daydreaming about buying the apartment, moving back to

Argentina, and getting a job teaching English or working at a supermarket, when a kid of about sixteen snatched the phone right out of my hand and ran into oncoming traffic and almost got hit over by a truck. I was going to chase him, but I was too lazy. I'm honestly loving not having a phone. I'm disconnected and free. Although I am dying to text Mom and Dad right now to tell them I love them and fill them in on what's going on inside Chichi's apartment.

Remember my filthy rich great-aunt Chichi? The one who owned one of Argentina's biggest transportation companies, who used to invite me, Rita, and a bunch of poor women who owed her favors to watch her model her expensive outfits and fur coats? The one who used to call her maid over by ringing a little bell? She's throwing a welcome party in my honor at her penthouse. The decor, which hasn't been touched since the 1970s, meaning it's gone out of style and fully come back into style again, includes a sunken living room with burnt-orange shag carpets and a wall-size painting of her face that makes her resemble Tommy Lee Jones but with long red hair.

Chichi is now in her nineties. She's one of the few family members left in Argentina I stay in touch with. She's bored and lonely and has tons of money to spend before she dies. (I think everyone who owed her favors is dead, and no one comes to visit anymore.) Plus, she just broke up with her boyfriend who was forty years younger and drove a taxi, and will use any excuse to have people over, so when I told her I was taking a solo trip back home, she said, "You're staying at my place, darling. And I'm throwing you a party. Invite whoever you want. I'll have it catered and hire a jazz trio." I told her a jazz trio wasn't necessary, but I wouldn't mind her inviting whoever she was still in touch with from either side of my family.

I didn't expect many people. I did a horrible job of staying in touch with elementary school friends over the years, and the other Argentines I was close to are dead or living abroad. But Chichi's apartment was packed. The first to arrive was Conchita, my singing instructor. We held each other and cried. I didn't want to let go. "Your mom wrote to me a few months ago to tell me that a TV show about your life was being made!" she said. "Do you remember that note I gave you before you left? I knew you'd conquer Hollywood!"

"It's true! I did it!" I answered. Then I quickly changed the subject because, a few weeks before the trip, I'd gotten a call from the network informing me that my show was getting killed and would not, in fact, be made, and I got so depressed I didn't get out of bed for a week straight. But I wasn't going to bum Conchita out with all of that.

My second cousin Damián (the one I hooked up with after a bar mitzvah) is also inside. He recently got a divorce and came with his preteen daughter who thinks I'm a celebrity. "She follows you on social media," Damián told me when he arrived. "She wants to be like you when she grows up." This comment somehow made me feel important and pathetic at the same time. Important because this Argentine child looked up to me. Pathetic because the validation from this preteen felt way too fucking good. Damián looks hot. Would fuck. I wonder what my life would be like if I lived here and married him and was a cool, hip stepmom to this young girl and made her lunches for school?

There's like twelve Yajias inside. Mostly my dad's cousins, who all look alike. But there's also a bunch of new Yajias. Baby Yajias I've never met, and young Yajias who don't know who I am. I see my dad's face in every single one of them, and it makes me want to cry. Everything makes me want to cry today. But that may also be because I've had too much wine and I'm on my period, something that I keep mentioning to everyone who comes up to talk to me and then instantly regrets it. There's one boy of about seven who looks *especially* like my dad. The resemblance is uncanny. His name is Kevin, and he has bad ADHD and knocked over one of Chichi's expensive Lladró figurines the second he arrived. I thought Chichi would get mad, but she looked at the boy and said, "Who cares?" Then she grabbed a different figurine and smashed it on the ground and called one of her maids to clean it up. What a stunning psycho. I had the thought that, since she doesn't have any children, maybe Chichi would leave me her fortune when she dies and I could move to her apartment in Argentina and be rich as hell and smash Lladró figurines all day. But that's neither here nor there. I went up to my dad's cousin to point out how much Kevin looked like dad. He chuckled to himself, leaned in, and whispered in my ear, "Kevin is actually adopted."

My grandfather Benjamín's only remaining brother is here. He looks just like him. When he walked in, I gave him a kiss on the cheek and looked at him with love. He looked back at me with a sour face and asked me why I was looking at him with pity. What a dick. Apparently, he has dementia and his wife just left him because she caught him fingering their maid. Classic. Very my family.

Another interesting guest was a man by the name of Daniel. Daniel is one of Pocho's nephews, whom I'd met many times during my youth. Daniel's face was bright red for some reason. He's one of those people who are constantly worked up about everything. He kept talking to me with his mouth full of focaccia and telling me how my grandpa Pocho fucked him over with money while spitting bread chunks all over me. Chichi walked up and asked me if Daniel was making me uncomfortable and offered to have him escorted out of her penthouse. "Absolutely not," I answered. Even the bad interactions are a dream come true. Even if this man was a trash compactor, he was a little bit of Pocho.

I take the last drag of my cigarette and throw it off the balcony, watching it fall twenty-one stories until it disappears. For a second, I imagine my body falling off the balcony and dying in Argentina, and the idea doesn't displease me. I start laughing alone at the number of times I've imagined various iterations of my life (and death) in Argentina during this trip: the one where I move into Nilda's apartment and start working at a supermarket, the one where I marry my cousin, the one where I inherit Chichi's fortune, the one where I fall off the balcony and die. These are just the ones I've had today. (Yesterday I imagined the most insane one of all, the one where I never left Argentina and actually became the pop icon I had set out to be.) I open the sliding doors from the balcony and walk back into Chichi's apartment and make eye contact with Damián and wonder if I'm going to fuck him tonight. If I wasn't married, I most certainly would. A caterer hands me a flute of champagne because Chichi wants to make a toast for me. I look at all these people and ask myself: *In all honesty, would I really want to live in Argentina again?* I think about it for a moment. *Maybe? Probably not? Actually, I don't know. Not without Mom and Dad. Not without my sister. Not without my husband and my friends. But it's nice to have a choice.* We all raise our glasses as Chichi begins delivering a drunken, slurred speech about me: "To Tamara, the biggest star in this family," she says.

ACKNOWLEDGMENTS

First and foremost I want to thank my love, Pat. Your love and support are the number one reason why I believe in myself again. I love you with all my heart, babe. I want to thank my agent, Chad Luibl. You're a thoughtful and kind human and this book exists because of you! Truly. You realized I had a story to tell even before I did. Thank you to my amazing editors, Daniel Loedel and Amber Oliver, for taking a chance on me. Your notes and feedback were thoughtful and constructive and made me a better writer. Thank you to everyone at Bloomsbury for making this entire process an absolute joy. Thank you to my manager and friend, Aaron Bergman. I'm so lucky to have found you.

Thank you, Mom and Dad. I love you both so much. I know that reading this book may not be easy, but I hope you understand that telling this story saved me. I'm grateful for the love, the life, and the sense of humor you've given me. I'd choose you as parents a million times over. Thank you to my Nat. My best friend. What would I be without you? A disaster. You are my everything. Palmitos12.

Thank you to my Yajia family in Argentina: Lito, Ruthy, Alan, Kevin, and Nanu. To my aunt, Betina, who is probably crying as she reads this. To Mariela, mi tía cubana, and all of my parent's friends whom I LOVE as if they were family. Thank you to my O'Connor, Friedericy, Billingsley family. You've always made me feel at home. A special shout-out to Patrick, the best father-in-law in the world. Thank you to Sarita, Salvador, Coco, Luisa, Adriana, and Reisaleh. My guardian angels. You are always with me, everywhere I go.

Thank you to my friends, my chosen family. I wish I would have known, in my loneliest years, that you all existed. Thank you. Julie, my wonderful Julie. Thank you. Mattso, Natalie, Alex, Fede and Mati, Nick, Sarah, Angela, Clay, Macho, Jon, Anna, Greg, Miguel, Shaun, Brett, Eva, Eze, Tom, Roxie, Peter, Emma, Miranda, Madrid, El Garrobo. Thank you. Con Smell. Thank you, Lauren and Dana, who were a huge part of this book. Thank you, Nonna Sophia. Look at us. Thank you. Joel, my divalina. Thank you to my Luciano. My brother. My Laucha Perla Pezón. Thank you to my precious Andrew. I cherish you every day. Thank you, my sweet Jess. My root. I love you.

A special shout-out to Mark Duplass and Susanna Hoffs. Thank you for always lifting me up.

Thank you, Madonna Louise Veronica Ciccone.

And finally, I want to thank YOU for reading this book. Let's be friends.

A NOTE ON THE AUTHOR

Tamara Yajia is an Argentine writer, comedian, and ex–child star who authored the 2022 poetry collection *Poems I Wrote While Taking a Shit*. She also wrote and starred in a one-woman show, *Cumming of Age*. Tamara has written for *Click-Hole*, *Funny or Die*, and several comedy series, including *Acapulco*, *This Fool*, and the upcoming Netflix series *Strip Law*. She lives in Los Angeles with her husband and her dog, Odie.